'Tis the Season

Compiled and Edited by Terri Kalfas

GRACE
PUBLISHING

Verses marked ESV are taken from *The Holy Bible, English Standard Version*®, © 2001 by Crossway, a publishing ministry of Good News Publishers. ESV Text Edition: 2025.

Verses marked HCSB are taken from the *Holman Christian Standard Bible*, Copyright © 1999, 2000, 2002, 2003, 2009 by Holman Bible Publishers, Nashville Tennessee. All rights reserved.

Verses marked KJV are taken from the *King James Version* of the Bible.

Verses marked MSG are taken from *The Message* Copyright © 1993, 2002, 2018 by Eugene H. Peterson.

Verses marked NIV are taken from the *Holy Bible, New International Version*®, NIV® Copyright ©1973, 1978, 1984, 2011 by Biblica, Inc.® Used by permission. All rights reserved worldwide.

Verses marked NKJV are taken from the *New King James Version*®. Copyright © 1982 by Thomas Nelson. Used by permission. All rights reserved.

Verses marked NLT are taken from *Holy Bible, New Living Translation*, copyright © 1996, 2004, 2015 by Tyndale House Foundation. Used by permission of Tyndale House Publishers, Inc., Carol Stream, Illinois 60188. All rights reserved.

Royalties for this book are donated to Samaritan's Purse.

'Tis the Season

ISBN-13: 978-1-60495-111-0

Copyright © 2025 by Grace Publishing House, Broken Arrow, Oklahoma. Published in the U.S.A. by Grace Publishing House. All rights reserved. No part of this book may be reproduced in any form or by any electronic or mechanical means, including information storage and retrieval systems, without permission in writing, except as provided by U.S.A. Copyright law.

From Samaritan's Purse

We so appreciate your donating royalties from the sale of the books in the *Divine Moments* series to Samaritan's Purse.

What a blessing that you would think of us! Thank you for your willingness to bless others and bring glory to God through your literary talents. Grace and peace to you.

Our Mission Statement

Samaritan's Purse, a nondenominational evangelical Christian organization provides spiritual and physical aid to hurting people around the world.

Since 1970, Samaritan's Purse has helped victims of war, poverty, natural disasters, disease, and famine with the purpose of sharing God's love through His Son, Jesus Christ.

Go and do likewise.
Luke 10:37

You can learn more by visiting our website at
samaritanspurse.org

Dedicated to Yvonne Lehman and the many authors
who so generously contribute their stories
to all of the books in the *Divine Moments* series.

Table of Contents

1. *Let There Be Light* Sherri R. Mewha 7
2. *The Gold Box* Sue Briggs 11
3. *Rock, Paper, Scissors* Tina Hurdt 14
4. *The Christmas Tree Skirt* Vicki H. Moss 17
5. *'Twas the Season of Advent* Xavia Arndt Sheffield 22
6. *Christmas at the Summit* Wendy C. Brown 27
7. *An Invitation for Christms* Brenda Poinsett 31
8. *The Christmas Trip to the Principal's Office* Anne Foley Rauth .. 37
9. *Lost and Found* Bonnie Evans 40
10. *The Tree* Maureen Miller 45
11. *Let's Make This a Banner Year!* Lydia E. Harris 49
12. *The Joy of an Unexpected Gift* Lorilyn Roberts 51
13. *It's Curtains for This Angel!* Annmarie B. Tait 54
14. *A Hole Full of Blessings* Judith Martin Harman 59
15. *The Gift of Christmas Visitors* Jan Elder 66
16. *Glory Be* Dee Bowlin 69
17. *Making Space for Christmas* J.J. LeVan 72
18. *Sweet Happy* Sharilynn Hunt 76
19. *Kiss the Cook* Connie K. Pombo 80
20. *The Stables* Kay S. Walsh 84
21. *The Story of Christmas* David Sowards 86

22. *The Mrs. Claus Blessing – A Fictional Christmas Tale*
    Ane Mulligan 88
23. *Mary's Mom – An Empty Nest Christmas Tale* Karen Cook 95
24. *Silent Night with Blue Eyes* Stacey Longo Graham 101
25. *Location, Location, Location* Lori Williams 104
26. *The Bracelet Promise* Carmen Leal 107
27. *Marry Christmas from Moldova* Terri Elders 112
28. *Wrappings* Joanna K. Harris 117
29. *Swaddling Clothes* Suzanne D. Nichols 119
30. *It Started with Bananas* Cecil Taylor 122
31. *Christmas on a Mountain Farm* Victoria Barker 126
32. *Favorite Christmas Tradition* Ben Cooper 130
33. *Remember the Child* Leigh Ann Thomas 133
34. *Alone for Christmas?* Barbara D'Antoni Diggs 135
35. *How to Cope Through the Season Alone* Donna Wyland 139
36. *A Very Different Christmas* April G. Pope 143
37. *A Priceless Gift for a Single Mom* Christina Ryan Claypool ... 145
38. *Letting Go of Christmas* Rhett Wilson, Sr. 151
39. *Putting Christmas Away* Norma C. Mezoe 154
40. *Jesus Christ – the Same Yesterday, Today, and December 26th*
    Thea Williams 155
41. *The Lambing Season* Susan M. Watkins 159

ABOUT THE AUTHORS 167

~ 1 ~
Let There Be Light!

Sherri R. Mewha

The people who walked in darkness have seen a great light;
those who dwelt in a land of deep darkness, on them has light shone.

Isaiah 9:2 ESV

We lay on the floor, flat on our backs, heads tucked under the lower branches of the rotating silver-aluminum Christmas tree. As we stared through the tree's silver arms, our eyes fixed on the ceiling, we shifted slightly now and then to watch the color dance on the walls.

It was pure magic.

The color wheel slowly rotated its four colors — red, green, gold, blue. Its lights reflected from branch to branch as they bounced off the silver and hot-pink ornaments, creating rainbows on every surface, including our upturned faces. Magic indeed.

It was the early 1960s. Aluminum Christmas trees were still novel in our neighborhood, and we had bought one. I thought it was the most beautiful thing I had ever seen. The lights and colors were enchanting. Lying on the floor of the living room to watch the Christmas lights became a much-loved tradition in our home. I must admit that now I am satisfied watching the Christmas lights from the comfort of my cozy armchair.

Today, Christmas lights are everywhere. They line the streets of our downtowns, replace the fallen leaves on bare branches, outline our houses, and line our sidewalks. If there's the remotest hint of darkness, never fear, lights can be strung!

Christmas — The Season of Lights!

For many, the "Season of Lights" is a time for family, gift-giving, sharing, kindness, and hope. Whether the celebration is Christmas, Hanukkah, Kwanzaa, or the winter solstice, when the longest night of the year takes place, light is a focal point of the season's celebrations.

The phrase "Season of Lights" should carry a much richer and more profound meaning for the Christian.

On Day One of the creation of our world, God proclaimed, *"Let there be light," and there was light. And God saw that the light was good. And God separated the light from the darkness* (Genesis 1:3-4 ESV). God's first gift to humanity, aside from Himself, was light. And He has been bringing the light ever since.

How beautiful is that!

At times, it seems the darkness of the world threatens to stamp out the light. There was such a time for the people of Israel. It had been over four hundred years since God's people had received a message from God. No doubt, it was long enough to make Israel wonder if God had forgotten about them.

Then in a manger in Bethlehem, the Light of the World broke through the darkness to be born as a tiny babe. The long-awaited Messiah arrived. God had not forgotten His people. (Luke 2:1-21)

And the world has never been the same.

The people who walked in darkness have seen a great light; those who dwelt in a land of deep darkness, on them has light shone. (Isaiah 9:2 ESV)

When we look around our world today, it may seem at times that the darkness is winning — war, corruption, injustice, illness, poverty, and evil run rampant.

Yes, the darkness threatens, but God's Word speaks Truth. The darkness may try to extinguish the light, but God's faithful stand firm and fight back, empowered by the Holy Spirit.

When we enjoy the lights of Christmas, we should remind ourselves that it is *God* who is the Giver of Light. He sent His Light to live among us. God gave Himself so that He might shine in us and through us.

God is light, and in Him is no darkness at all. (1 John 1:5 ESV)

It is no coincidence that on one of the darkest days of the year, Christians celebrate the birth of Jesus, the Messiah and the Light of the World.

Throughout Scripture, we see God reveal Himself as a beacon of light. His light calls us to Him. The Light of God:

- leads us as it did for the Children of Israel in the wilderness (Exodus 13:21).
- identifies us as His (Exodus 10:23).
- guards and guides us (Psalm 27:1, Isaiah 42:60).
- is the armor in which He wraps us for the battles of life (Romans 13:12).
- is life-giving (John 8:12).

And finally, it is the Light that we, God's light-bearers, are to share with all the world.

In the same way, let your light shine before others, so that they may see your good works and give glory to your Father who is in heaven. (Matthew 5:15 ESV)

In His light, we find our purpose. We have been called out of darkness to become light bearers — taking the light of Jesus to those who still wander in the darkness without God.

You are a chosen race, a royal priesthood, a holy nation, a people for His own possession, that you may proclaim the excellencies of Him who called you out of darkness into His marvelous light. (1 Peter 2:9 ESV)

During these days of celebration, as you light your candles, sit in the glow of a burning blaze beside the fireplace, or enjoy the lights that dress your Christmas tree, focus your thoughts on the Giver of Light. Remember the One Who is the Light of the World. And never forget that The Light that He has given you is a precious gift to share with those still walking in darkness.

May the joy of God's light shine brightly in your heart throughout the Christmas Season and every day of the New Year.

God, who said, "Let light shine out of darkness," has shone in our hearts to give the light of the knowledge of the glory of God in the face of Jesus Christ.

2 Corinthians 4:6 ESV

For at one time you were darkness, but now you are light in the Lord. Walk as children of light.

Ephesians 5:8 ESV

~ 2 ~
The Gold Box

Sue Briggs

For the first time in my life, I was not excited about Christmas. When I looked at the lovely nativity set my sister had made us, my thoughts went to my three-year-old daughter and to a baby who was born to be crucified. When I gazed at our small but lovely tree with the miscellaneous shiny ornaments, ropes of pearls, multicolored lights, and small angel on top, I thought of the big, beautiful Christmas trees of my childhood that we loved sharing with our friends and family.

The few gifts under this tree brought back memories of exciting giftwrap nights with my family. These gifts I had wrapped alone, using leftover paper. I felt guilty that some of them were from garage sales or a discount store. I was not eager for the next night of lonely giftwrapping.

I thought of our daughter having no one but us with whom to share Christmas morning excitement.

My husband and I did not know many people with small children. I missed my professional job and felt totally inadequate as a mother. I was exhausted trying to be everything and do everything for my child. Our nearby relatives had made it plain that they did not want to share Christmas with us. I felt lonely for my husband and child being rejected by relatives. The relatives who were interested were too far away to visit. I was crushed with the feeling that my husband and I could not provide our child with the exciting, family-centered Christmases we had both enjoyed.

To help my child have playmates, to meet some other parents, and to help myself cope I had started going to a facility called the Family Growth Center in our town. Supervised play was provided for children while adults met to talk about whatever was on their minds. This particular week, exhaustion, despair, and worry about Christmas were on everyone's mind. We were not a jolly group.

As we ended for the day, our leaders surprised each of us with a small gift — and I do mean surprised us! For the first time that day, we were all smiling and made hasty plans to get together for something fun. My gift was a little bottle of cologne, given to me in a gold box with a red bow. Until I received that, I had not realized how much I needed a beautifully-presented, frivolous gift. I knew it was not an exotic, expensive perfume. It didn't matter. It was in a lovely box, and it smelled good. It reminded me that although I was not a discouraged mother, I was also a woman. I could wear the cologne for my husband. I could wear it for the little gathering we were quickly planning.

God used this gift to help me see that sometimes people need something special . . . maybe a little frivolous, pretty, feminine (or masculine). I thought of my widowed mother, and from then on I made sure she got something a little special, a little feminine, a little pretty each year.

God helped me take a fresh look around me. I bought some beautiful blue Christmas wrap with pictures of little kittens on it (who looked remarkably like our cats) to use along with my older Christmas wrap. I reached out to a single mother with a preteen daughter who was also having a difficult time and invited them to come wrap gifts with us. Even my husband got involved in giftwrapping. At first we all felt a little tentative, then my husband said something funny, I said "Bozo," and we all started laughing and had a great time.

Yes, Christmas morning was still a little lonely, but God helped me focus on some good things. My husband, daughter and I were together. We had a nice Christmas dinner. My daughter enjoyed her gifts and did not give a rip that some were from garage sales. We visited on the phone with the relatives who wanted to be with us but couldn't. Looking at our nativity set, I remembered the birth of Christ led to our redemption.

Over the years I was able to buy for more people. For nursing home patients, for people going through a rough time, I made sure to include something special. Gifts didn't need to be expensive to be nice. They could be inexpensive cologne, a small but pretty box of candy, a fancy handkerchief.

Sometimes Christmas seasons still carried some loneliness, but I remembered that cologne in a beautiful gold box with a red bow, and God helped me focus on other people and on being more positive.

~ 3 ~
Rock, Paper, Scissors

Tina Hurdt

It was a chilly Wednesday night in December of 2013. I was driving children home from church in the church van. It was our last meeting before Christmas, so I was handing out goodie bags to each child.

My last stop was the home of two girls, ages eight and five. The oldest was very shy, but so sweet-spirited. The youngest, a little more social. The girls had parents who loved them yet could not conquer their addiction to drugs. Mom had been in the hospital and Dad had just lost his job. A sad situation, but these girls were very loving despite their circumstances.

I pulled into their driveway and walked around to open the side door. I handed them each a treat bag and wished them a Merry Christmas. The older girl said, "Wait, Ms. Tina. I have something for you too!" Off she darted toward the house. Her little sister, sitting beside me in the van doorway, simply shrugged her shoulders. I thought to myself, "How can she have a gift for *me*? I knew our church had recently furnished their Christmas gifts and food for the holiday.

Moments later, she came skipping out of the house. In the glow of the streetlight, I could see that she was carrying a bag and wearing a huge smile on her face. She offered me the bag and said, "This is for you." The bag was tattered and worn, and pieces of packaging tape had been crudely cut to hold the bag together.

I smiled back and asked, "Can I open it now?" She chewed on her lip and quickly nodded her approval. I looked into the bag and took out the sheet of crumpled notebook paper that served as tissue paper. As I peered deeper into the bag, a big lump formed in my throat. The bag was full of *rocks*.

I looked up at her and asked, "Are these really for me?" She was nearly beside herself with pride.

She rocked back and forth on her feet and said "Uh-huh. I looked for the rocks that I thought you would like. They're all different." Her little sister added "'Took her forever."

Rolling her eyes at her younger sister, she looked at me and asked, "Do you like them, Ms. Tina?"

With tears in my eyes, I managed to squeak out "They're the most beautiful rocks I've ever seen. Thank you so much! Can I give you a hug?" She nodded, and I hugged both girls and sent them into the house. Even from behind in the dim light, I could see their smiles as they talked to each other, walking down the driveway.

I closed the van door and walked around and climbed into the driver's side. For a moment, I just sat there. Stunned. What had just happened? Then I realized I had experienced the true meaning of Christmas — an innocent little gift from the heart. This little girl had just given me the best she had. She wasn't worried about the cost, the lack of supplies, or even the packaging. She had used rocks, paper, and scissors to create something I would treasure for the rest of my life. Isn't that exactly what God did for us? He offered His best in hopes that we would accept and treasure that very special Gift.

This Christmas, I encourage you to *make* time to be alone with God. Thank Him for the most wonderful Gift of His Son, Jesus Christ. A Gift that gives every day — a Gift that blesses every day; the Gift of an eternal relationship we should treasure every day of our lives.

~ 4 ~
The Christmas Tree Skirt

Vicki H. Moss

Christmas traditions were always important to me. Not only did I celebrate the Christ child by attending church services, I loved decorating for the holidays.

Many Christmases ago, I longed to sew up a special Christmas skirt for the tree that would stand before the window in my first home's dining room. It was to be a special Christmas tree skirt, not just a white sheet to look like snow, but one that could be passed down in the family, along with Mother's Red Velvet cake recipe, for many years to come.

With a pattern chosen — how can you go wrong with making a basic circle design — I selected fabric for the pie-shaped wedges that would make up the circle of the skirt: green velvet, red velvet, and a green and red cotton plaid that would be sewn in between the solid green and red velvets. The plaid fabric would also match the large bows that would be wired together for a tree topper with long streamers hanging down to grace the tree — making for a traditional red, green, and plaid decorated tree for my family's great room. The tree ornaments were to be red and green with bubble lights bubbling the same colors. School handmade ornaments could always be added in future years, along with any lovely ornaments I found while traveling.

I found a beautiful white lace to sew down the seams to make the skirt pop and stand out, and then made double layered red bows to be sewn at the bottom of every seam.

More cloth was bought than what was needed, so I could make Christmas dresses that matched the Christmas tree skirt — surely I would have a daughter one day. So I bought more cloth to have one sleeveless dress made from the green velvet. I added pearls on the shoulders along with a white laced strip of trim across the bodice seam.

Another dress was made of red velvet, and a third was made of the plaid cloth. A white cotton blouse with a Peter Pan collar would be worn beneath all three dresses, or sometimes, depending on the weather, a warm white turtleneck.

After I had a little girl, a cousin came over to see the drapes I'd made to hang from the ceiling around the baby bed. She peeked into the nursery's closet and laughed. "Hey, you have every size in here for her until she gets to high school but where's the prom dress? She has everything else!" Of course she was exaggerating and being her comedic self, but I confess that when I saw a darling outfit that was really cute — and even better, on sale — I bought it knowing a baby girl would grow into it.

After the dresses were made, I started on the Christmas tree skirt.

To quote an old cliché, had I "bitten off more than I could chew?"

There was no problem assembling and sewing the topper. However, it was lined and that made two layers of fabric to sew through when attaching the lace strips along the seams. Plus, velvet is thicker than cotton plaid and I wasn't prepared for the intense struggle with running all that fabric beneath the foot attachment on my sewing machine.

I had a plan and had spent the money and I would not be defeated.

I managed to make the tree skirt like someone would eat an elephant. One bite at a time. When finished, the tree skirt was beautiful. After showing it to some friends, comments were made: "Make me one. That's the prettiest Christmas tree skirt I've ever seen!"

"Not on your life! This is one of hardest projects I've ever worked on and it had better last a lifetime and another generation's lifetime because I'm never making another one of these skirts — ever again!"

When Thanksgiving rolled around and the turkey had been eaten and all the decorations were put away, out came the Christmas decorations. Up went the balled live spruce tree, and out came the Christmas tree skirt after the tree's limbs were decorated. And that's when I started one of my family's first traditions. We had to try on the Christmas tree skirt, tell the year, our age and if in school, the grade, and then give the skirt a big twirl in front of a video camera. Only then would the Christmas tree skirt take its place beneath the tree — all ready for colorfully wrapped packages.

When my daughter married and moved to San Francisco, California, I decided it was time the Christmas tree skirt should go with her along with her English bulldog named Duchess Tula

Belle of Oxford, Mississippi, aka "Tootie." Both, when shipped to California, were less for me to deal with. Let the younger folk put up a Christmas tree and host Christmas dinner if they weren't flying home.

Fortunately, from then on the Christmas tree was already assembled and decorated before I arrived to celebrate Christmas so I didn't have to participate in the skirt twirling anymore. I did buy a beautiful white cake stand for the newlyweds in San Fran so my child could also make Mother's regal Red Velvet cake.

One year, I received a video from my daughter and her husband. By this second year of marriage the kids had moved to Denver, Colorado. A guy friend of theirs happened to be visiting them and Tootie when they were putting up their Christmas tree. My son-in-love was reminded by his traditional Southern wife who loves traditions, "Don't forget, we can't put the Christmas tree skirt under the tree unless we try it on and give it a twirl like we did last year."

Their guest was amused. And curious. "What's all this about twirling a Christmas tree skirt?"

My child filled him in. "Mom started a family tradition years ago and when I was little, each year before the skirt went beneath the tree after the ornaments were hung, we each had to put the skirt on, state the year, our full name, our age, our school grade, and then had to give the skirt a big twirl."

The guest laughed and jumped up. "Hey, I want to participate — I'm next!"

After that second Christmas, the kids headed back to Tennessee where they'd met and where my child grew up. From then on, I once again became a part of the Christmas decoration event only now, there are three girls trying on that same Christmas tree skirt I made forty-two years ago. Each one, after stating the year, her full name, and her age, tries to beat her sisters with the biggest skirt twirl.

And I — well I enjoy the skirt twirling from across the room. And doubt that I'll ever get that skirt around my waist in the future, unless I stop eating Red Velvet cake that my daughter now makes every year to continue her grandmother's Christmas tradition from long ago.

When it comes time for the Christmas tree skirt to be passed down, things will get interesting. Maybe the granddaughter who gets the skirt needs to host the dinner and bake the cake!

~ 5 ~
'Twas the Season of Advent

Xavia Arndt Sheffield

'Twas the season of Advent,
that time of the year
When candles and wreaths
begin to appear.

A circle of green
shaped like God's love,
Eternal, unending,
His gift from above.

Four colored candles
in purple or blue,
Stand tall all around
with a white one, too.

Each candle, a symbol
to give us some clues,
And tell us the story
of God's good news.

As we all settle in
to wait for God's Son,
We start to learn
how salvation was won.

We light the first candle
for prophets of old,
And learn that Christ's birth
had been foretold.

The prophet Isaiah
and Micah too,
Tell of God's plan
to make everything new.

From the family of Jesse
shall come a new shoot,
A sign to the people
shall grow out of his root.

His light will shine
on the darkness we're in,
It will shine brightly
to free us from sin.

We light the next candle
for John, who first came,
To prepare all the people
for Jesus' great name.

To the priest Zechariah,
an angel appeared
And gave him a message
but he greatly feared.

"Do not be afraid
for your prayer has been heard,
A son will be born,
for this is God's word."

On Elizabeth, too,
this blessing was poured,
And John was great
in the sight of the Lord.

We light the pink candle
to tell you the joy,
Of the shepherds and Mary
on the birth of her boy.

The angel Gabriel
appeared to a maid,
And told her God's plan
and then Mary prayed:

"I am the Lord's servant,
I will do what is right,
For I have found favor
in God's holy sight."

An angel told Joseph
God's will would be done,
That Mary was chosen
to give birth to God's son.

The shepherds were watching
their flocks that night,
And the glory of God
shone on them so bright.

An angel of God
appeared to them,
And brought them good news
for all women and men.

No longer afraid,
they rushed into town,
And finding the child,
told all those around.

The last colored candle,
the candle of love,
Is also of angels
come down from above.

Joining the angel
with voices all raised,
The heavenly host
proclaimed God's praise:

"Glory to God
in heaven's great height.
Peace to all people,
good will on this night."

Four times in our story
at just the right hour,
Angels appeared
to reveal God's power.

The white Christ candle,
its light all aglow
Shines forth God's promise
for all people to know.

His Word became flesh
in a baby that night,
And our darkness cannot
extinguish His light.

That light is our life
God's gift to us all,
Through all of the people
who answered God's call.

The best is for last,
what God has in store,
Advent means "coming"
and He's coming once more!

~ 6 ~
Christmas at the Summit

Wendy C. Brown

A bah-humbugger sort of week had already riled my hackles, and now I had to haul the family off to the Christmas parade. The kids needed layers, coats, gloves, and tissues, while what I needed was a vacation in Hawaii.

"Mom, where's my lucky reindeer?"

"Mom, she won't let me borrow her socks."

"Mom, my nose is running again."

"Mom, we can't be late for the parade."

Well, "Mom" could handle everything if we would give her a second to think! Think... my thoughts at that time were attempts to grasp the overwhelming sense of Christmas imagination I had long since lost.

With the car full of coats and coveralls, a thermos of warm chocolate-raspberry cocoa, and plastic bags for all the candy they throw on the street, we loaded up, buckled up, everything but shut-ted up! A headache had already settled into my brain and began throbbing to the rhythm of Jingle Bells chiming in three different keys from the back seat, including one version about a bow-legged cowboy.

How I wish we could celebrate the birth of Christ at a quiet manger with a few close friends! I thought. *No such hope of Christ appearing this year.* My Christmas greeting changed from "Merry Christmas" to "Survive the Holidays."

This was just our second year attending the parade, so we chose to park and then walk to the same spot we stood last year. We wove through the crowd of merry-makers, intending to maintain the same number of kids at all times. My husband and two of our children disappeared, and I turned just in time to see them following the mobile Free Hot Chocolate sign. So, I stood with my hands in my pockets, my eyes on the ground. The wind was the coldest it had been in a while.

Perched in a tense and distant state, I wondered why we chose to stand in front of the Summit. People who live there aren't like us. The whole building pours out onto the street when the parade starts. Many who live there have varying degrees of mental and emotional disabilities, and you never know what one of them will say or do.

My family returned just as I began to imagine Stephen King material coming to life before me, and just in time to see the giant banner that introduces the parade being marched around the corner. I was stuck.

For twenty minutes, I yanked on hats to reposition the children so they were standing on the sidewalk. Dive-bombing for candy in front of large rescue vehicles and reindeer floats is not acceptable to Mom or the police.

I whispered to myself, "Nope. No Christ in Christmas this year."

The words had barely left my mouth when a blood-curdling

scream jumped from a page of those King books right behind me. My neck ducked like lightning into my coat collar, and I felt two inches tall. Shivers raced up my legs, crossed the spiny expanse of my back, and smacked me upside the head. Unbeknownst to me, the Christmas spirit had arrived.

"He's coming!" She screamed again, "He's coming. He's coming. He's coming!"

She grabbed the lapels of my coat, gave them a shake, and whispered a scream I could smell, "He's coming." White hair flowed long and scraggly down her shoulders and back. In the freezing temperatures, she wore only jeans, a dirty sweatshirt, and mismatched gloves. With fiery gumption and sprite-like leaps, she danced around me, and I saw my entire life pass before my Scroogy eyes.

Throughout the rest of the parade, she continued to dance around in my personal space, pointing at cute little puppies wearing red tutus, snow globe floats, cheery green elves, and tractors with big red bows. At every entry to pass in the parade, she screamed with delight. And every few entries, she would grab my shoulders and whisper that odorous shout, "He's coming!"

Before long, I felt this giggle begin deep in my socks somewhere. As much as I hoped it would stay there, I found it inching upward. In minutes, I couldn't contain myself, and the silliest sound burst out of my mouth. With tears in my eyes, I began to laugh.

My Christmas sprite then picked up a tootsie roll from the street and brought it to me. Looking right in my eyes, she gave me the chocolate and said, "Merry Christmas, He's coming!"

As soon as the words came out of her mouth, she stopped and grabbed her chest. My laughing ceased. I thought she was having a heart attack right beside me. Her eyes remained open, though, and with great emotion, she shook her head, "He's not coming . . . ."

I bent closer, pressing my ear close to her mouth, hoping breath was still coming out. Then she squealed and blared like an air horn. "He's not coming! He's here! He's here!"

Sure enough, Santa had just made the corner, only a few feet away. The imagination of Christmas swept me away on Santa's sleigh as he passed. My giggles turned to red-faced belly laughter as the kids now wondered more at their mirth-filled mother than at Santa. That night, the woman with no name and a simple home at the Summit transformed me as she made her way up the street following Santa. She lit the parade with her shouts of "It's him! "It's really him!"

She soon returned and grabbed my hand with a gentle, almost reverent squeeze. Circled by a new group of Summit friends, I watched in awe as Santa rode into the distance, smiling and shouting a merry "Ho-Ho-Ho!"

I knew then, as she whispered one more time, "He's here," that Christ had been there all the time, just waiting for me to share in the imagination of Christmas at the Summit.

~ 7 ~
An Invitation for Christmas

Brenda Poinsett

"Don't expect much" regularly popped out of my mouth the year my husband had been unemployed for six months. Bob had resumed working in November, but he hadn't been working long enough for us to get caught up with the accumulated bills. We didn't want to add to our debt so we decided to spend very little for Christmas.

We bought a marked-down Christmas tree with a very crooked trunk for ten dollars. While our sons decorated it, they began talking about Christmas morning when they would open gifts from Bob and me. *Hmm,* I thought, *I had better nip this anticipation in the bud.* I said, "Now, boys, don't expect much for Christmas this year."

When they watched television and saw those commercials especially designed to make children "want," they dreamed aloud about what they would get. I interrupted their dreams with, "Remember, boys, don't expect much this Christmas."

When their friend Bruce came over to play with six-year-old Ben, they talked about what they were going to get. As they drove their trucks over the carpet, they chattered about the toys they wanted. When Bruce left, I said, "Now, Ben, don't expect much for Christmas."

I said "don't expect much" so many times that I felt like a new Christmas character was developing. She was The Christmas Damper — a character that would take her place right a long with Ebenezer Scrooge and The Grinch. The minute she heard boys and girls expressing their Christmas wishes, she threw water on them. Her goal was to put out the fires of Christmas expectation.

Jim, almost a teen-ager, took to spending a lot of time in his room with the door closed. Joel, two years younger, was listless. Saying he didn't have anything to do, he leaned on my desk while I tried to work. Ben acted babyish. He kept wanting to sit on my lap like he did when he was smaller. A Christmas gloom settled over our house.

If anyone had told me in November that this would happen, I would have said, "Not at my house!" I had been certain that having little money to spend would not affect the quality of our celebration because every year I worked at emphasizing meaning. This year, though, the advent candles no longer held an attractive glow. Our daily December devotions, an activity the boys always welcomed, no longer held their interest.

When our pastor preached a sermon blaming the loss of meaning on the hustle and bustle of Christmas, I said, "Bah! Humbug!" I had not bought one ribbon, one gift tag or one piece of wrapping paper. We weren't caught up in the hustle and bustle of the holidays, but something was missing from our Christmas.

I was relieved when a real estate agent that I sometimes worked for called. Carileen said, "I've decided to have an open house. I want to show my new home to my customers. Would you bake the cookies, prepare the punch, and serve them at my open house?"

I welcomed the job. *Perhaps baking thirty dozen cookies and preparing punch will get my thoughts off our gloomy Christmas.* It did while I shopped for the ingredients. But when I rolled the dough for the sugar cookies, I thought of my mother, five-hundred miles away. At that moment, she was probably also baking. During the holidays, people came and went at Mother's house, and she offered pie and coffee to each one. Warmth permeated her home. I wished we could go home so we could experience that warmth and escape the gloom at our house.

How did Mother achieve that holiday warmth? How did she develop an atmosphere where people felt they could stop by without being asked? Did it take years of living in a community for people to feel that comfortable? Did it happen only when relatives lived nearby? Our family had no relatives close by, and we hadn't lived in our community very long.

Thinking about the warmth in my mother's home made the Christmas gloom hang even heavier.

The morning of Carileen's open house, I wrote in my journal, "There's something wrong this Christmas. Sadness prevails. My family is not excited or happy about Christmas, and yet I don't want it to be this way. I want something more because Christmas is significant."

"Lord Jesus," I prayed, "I have always tried to honor you at Christmas. Help me to identify what the problem is and help me see how to correct it."

I loaded the cookies, the serving trays, the punch, and the

punch bowl and went to Carileen's. I kept the punch bowl filled and cookies on the trays while her customers came and went. Hearing their laughter and talk, I felt a warmth — a warmth similar to what permeated my mother's house. At Mother's, they came and went because they knew her. At Carileen's, people came and went because they were invited. If I wanted to create warmth at my own home, perhaps I needed to invite people.

When I got home, I took a deep breath and said to Bob and the boys, "I have an idea. I know this sounds crazy, but let's have an open house."

"No one would come," Bob said. "Everyone we know will be spending Christmas with their families."

"Perhaps we could ask them to stop by Christmas Eve afternoon for a few minutes on the way to wherever they are going," I countered.

"But you have been reminding us all month how little money we have. How can we afford an open house?" asked Jim, with his anger clearly evident.

"People won't eat much if they are on their way to some place where they will be eating. Besides, I learned this week that a five-pound sack of flour makes a lot of cookies. We could serve cookies and punch. Instead of an elaborate fruit punch, I could serve that kool-aid/orange juice combination I make for you in the summer."

"What about postage?" said Bob.

"Even if we could afford the postage, people would not get an invitation in time since Christmas is just a few days away. Let's hand-deliver them. We could give them out at church tomorrow, and you kids can take them to school. You can invite whomever you want."

Their eyes lit up. Together, they said, "Let's do it!"

"I'll need your help if we're going to get everything ready in time," I told them.

Bob, our resident poet, said, "I'll make the invitations. A poem is already forming in my head."

We gave out invitations at church the next day, and the boys took them to school on Monday. What fun we had handing out invitations to people we knew well, to people we wanted to know better, and to people in situations like our own!

On Monday and Tuesday after school, we baked cookies. On Wednesday, with no school, Jim, Joel, Ben, and I cleaned house. The weather was unseasonably warm so we opened the windows. We polished the furniture with lemon oil and shook the rugs. Anyone driving by our country home would have thought spring house cleaning was taking place!

Finally, at thirty minutes before time for the open house to begin on Thursday, we had everything ready. The boys kept opening the front door to look down the road to see if anyone was coming. After several looks, they sat down. Joel said, "Can you believe it? Can you believe we finally have everything ready?"

I used that moment to remind them that Jesus came in the fullness of time when God had everything ready (Galatians 4:4). I said, "God, the Father, planned and made special arrangements for Jesus' birth. God picked out a name. He chose a birthplace. He prepared the people by promising them from time to time that Jesus would come. Now that we understand what it takes to get ready for something important, let's thank God for preparing the world for Jesus' coming."

We said our prayer, and the doorbell rang. The first guest was arriving! During the afternoon thirty-seven people came — just the right number. Their coming and going stretched out over the afternoon so there was lots of leisurely conversation. While most were on their way to other places, they seemed to enjoy the relaxed atmosphere of our home. While they were there, warmth arrived and lingered long after the last guest departed.

The gloom had departed earlier. From the time we started planning our open house, the boys no longer talked about what they were going to *get* for Christmas. Gifts no longer mattered. In a year when we didn't have much, we learned that celebration matters. Some hustle and bustle is appropriate for celebrating Jesus' birth.

~ 8 ~

The Christmas Trip to the Principal's Office

Anne Foley Rauth

I wanted to become an ostrich and bury my head in the sand. (Until I learned they really don't do that.) Then I considered joining the FBI's Witness Protection program. (But I wasn't an informant seeking protection.) I finally decided I had to face the music and return the principal's telephone call.

It was early December, and our youngest son had been sent to the principal's office by his second-grade teacher. He had made three unkind comments throughout the week to three of his friends, one of whom was the principal's son.

"You look like a dummy with that haircut," was the third strike that week, for our usually very kind youngest son.

I was mortified and apologized profusely, promising to talk to our son that night.

When I picked him up that evening from after-school care, I decided to wait and see if he told me about his eventful visit. And I didn't have to wait long; his older brother was very excited to share the news with me. "Guess what? 'Topher got sent to the principal's office today!"

I, of course, acted shocked, stunned, and dismayed. I also told 'Topher that this was an unfortunate occurrence, as I'm sure that Santa's elves had raced off to tell Santa. I let that sink in for a minute before saying, "Perhaps it would also be a good idea to write an apology note to each of your friends?"

The apology letters were written in the very best second-grade handwriting he could muster up. They were heartfelt and would be delivered in person the next day.

This was a teachable moment, and I really wanted to make the most of this as I believe words are very powerful, and I wanted all of our boys to remember that "*words kill, words give life; they're either poison or fruit–you choose*" (Proverbs 18:21 MSG).

That same day, my husband had his early-morning Bible study, and I was reminded that one of the men attending was quite busy this time of year, "helping" Santa out by filling in for him at a local mall. With his beautiful grey beard and his comforting voice, if he were willing, this could really help drive home the lesson that words matter.

Several nights after the trip to the principal's office, my husband's phone rang with a video call. It was an unknown number, but the gentleman on the phone had a very familiar face. A red cap sat on his head, slightly covering his grey hair.

"I was wondering if a certain young man named 'Topher Rauth might be available?"

"Let me go get him for you," I calmly replied.

Our youngest son was so excited to receive a telephone call that he skipped into the parlor area, where my husband had his phone.

"Is that you, Topher?" the man said.

Topher gasped when he realized who was on the phone. He could not speak; all he could do was nod his head up and down.

"My elves told me something recently about you that I find very hard to believe," Santa calmly said. "They told me that you've said some unkind things to your friends recently, and I told them that I knew they had the wrong young man, because you are normally always kind and considerate to others, right? That's one way you shine the light of Jesus. You treat people like he would."

'Topher continued to be silent and was just profusely nodding his head.

"Well, I've got to get back to everyone's lists, so you keep up the good work and use kind words, okay, Topher?" Santa waved goodbye to all of us, hung up, and 'Topher said, "I'm sunk this Christmas."

"Topher, I believe that Santa knows you can and will do better. Let's write your letter to him, and you can tell him yourself."

As Topher sat down to craft his letter to Santa, he assured him that he would use kind words and looked up at me with his long eyelashes and said, "Mom, I will be better. Words really do matter."

He and I mailed the letter the very next day, and I could see he had a hopeful attitude. I guess Santa believed him, too, because there were gifts for him and a "keep up the good work" note under our tree on Christmas Day.

All of us know what we should do, but sometimes it takes a little encouragement to do the next right thing. Christmas is always a great time to start.

~ 9 ~

Lost and Found

Bonnie Evans

There wasn't any hint during the day that this Wednesday — November 19, 1980 — would be different than any other — that it would become every parent's worst nightmare or teach me lessons I'd never forget.

Just as I slid the last dumpling into the pot of chicken soup, five-year-old Melissa burst into the kitchen.

"I'm gonna get the newspaper, 'kay?"

"Matt, can you go with her?"

"I've got Royal Rangers tonight and gotta get this math done." My seven-year-old son was at the kitchen counter surrounded by homework.

I pointed a finger still caked in sticky dough and warned her, "Okay, but come right back! No lollygagging!"

Her blonde pigtails bobbed in agreement. I made a mental note to redo her hair before church as she banged the door into the outside wall on her way out.

We lived in a rural area, and our home was at the end of a long S-shaped driveway. This was the first time Missy would walk down to the two-lane country road by herself.

And — because it never occurred to me that Robert Dunton,

a recently released felon, would be passing in his station wagon, would spot Melissa, snatch her, toss her in his car, and drive away — I didn't worry.

We knew something was wrong right away: The walk took ten minutes, and she wasn't back in fifteen.

My husband hiked down and saw the mail untouched in its box and the newspaper lying on the gravel.

While Mike was gone, I checked her bedroom, closets, and other common hiding places in case she'd slipped into the house unnoticed.

Soon all three of us, as well as our few-and-far-between neighbors, were searching for her. We could hear voices calling her name as the sun sank. We could see flashlights bobbing and weaving among the trees and bushes.

We'd called for official help, but in those days, the police wouldn't take a missing person's report until the person had been gone twenty-four hours. It didn't matter if it was a five-year-old child, a teenager, or an elderly dementia patient.

Darkness fell and smothered all hope. Mike, Matt, and I stood in the garage staring at the night sky.

"Let's pray," Mike whispered as he reached for our hands.

His prayer was simple. a "God, help us find Melissa. Your eyes can see her, ours can't. Keep her safe and show us where to look."

With that, we turned back toward the open garage door. *Where do you look when you've already looked everywhere two, three, or four times?*

I was paralyzed with fear and indecision. Cruel images were seeping into my thoughts . . . Melissa lying unconscious in a ditch, coyotes roaming, cold fog settling onto her t-shirt and shorts.

The phone rang and broke the moment. Mike grabbed the outside handset, and I listened to his side of the conversation.

"Who is this?"

"Describe her."

"Who is this? Who am I talking to?"

Oh no! She's been kidnapped. This must be our ransom call, I thought. *What kind of price tag will they put on her head?*

I knew whatever they asked for, I would pay it.

The call wasn't the kidnapper but the California Highway Patrol. They'd found a little girl miles from our home and wanted to know if our daughter was missing. The dispatcher didn't have many facts but wanted us to meet the officer and the towheaded tyke where she'd been found.

Before we pulled off the freeway, we could see numerous police cars parked at all angles along the frontage road. Some still had their red-white-and-blue lights spinning.

I willed myself out of the car, wondering how Melissa could have gotten so far from home.

Mike looked for the person in charge while I scanned the scene looking for Melissa.

I spotted her in the back seat of a police car about the same time she saw me.

"Mommy, Mommy!" she mouthed while pounding on the locked door.

A sheriff let her out, and she jumped into my arms. I held her trembling body while she told me how Dunton had grabbed her and how she'd fought against his grasp.

"I just got out of prison for killing my wife and baby," he'd told her. "If you don't shut up, I'll kill you too."

"I'm never gonna see my mommy and daddy again," she'd sobbed back.

It appears Dunton became disoriented after snatching Melissa, and zagged around on curving roads for a while. Eventually, his turns landed him on a boulevard that would take him to the freeway.

Just as he turned toward a clean getaway, God gave us our miracle. A California Highway Patrolman pulled out behind Dunton's vehicle and noticed the battered car was missing a taillight. Officer Thompson admitted that since it was time to clock out, he'd decided to let the minor infraction slide. He later wrote in his report that when he passed the station wagon, it "veered suspiciously onto the shoulder of the road."

The evasive action, as well as the driver's averted glance, troubled him, so he decided to investigate using the taillight as an excuse. Inside the stopped vehicle, he found an unkempt young man and a child he hadn't seen while passing.

"He took me from my mommy and daddy," the little girl kept crying.

Dunton tried to excuse her tears, but the officer didn't believe him. Officer Thompson cuffed him and tried to find out who the youngster was and where she belonged.

Hours after the ordeal began, we knelt by Melissa's bed and thanked God for the grace He chose to send.

Public servants, family, and friends agreed: We would have never seen her again if God hadn't intervened.

Months later — after court appearances and sentencing, after we had returned to our normal work and school routines — I still struggled. Why had God allowed this?

One bright morning, clear of any streaks of ocean fog, He answered.

He took me back to the "ransom" call and my oath to buy my daughter back no matter what the cost. Then, He spoke to me in the quiet place where only He is heard.

"Would you really have paid any price to get her back?"

"Absolutely."

"Would you have sold your home? Sold everything you have and emptied your bank accounts?"

"Yes."

"Would you have borrowed money and gone into debt?"

"Yes, I'd have worked for the rest of my life to pay back loans."

Heaven paused before asking the final question.

"Would you have given your son?"

My heart recoiled. How could I choose one child over another, and why would God ask me to do such a thing?

Slowly, the truth of His heavenly analogy broke open.

For just moments, I could feel the depth of God's sacrifice and grief as He sent Jesus to a manger and Calvary's cross.

Jesus didn't just come. God gave. He gave one perfect child to release those taken and lost to His embrace. One perfect child to redeem all the others.

God so loved the world, that he gave his only begotten Son, that whosoever believeth in him should not perish, but have everlasting life.

John 3:16 KJV

~ 10 ~

The Tree

Maureen Miller

"Which one would be just right?" we ask,
We choose so carefully,
Then bring into our heart and home
The perfect Christmas tree.

All the family gathers 'round
The tree to dress with bling —
Some tinsel here, an ornament there,
Then carols we do sing.

Faithfully, the tree will stand
For several weeks or so.
"Turn on the lights!" the children cry,
Then faces shine within the glow.

Shopping done, the gifts are wrapped
And placed so thoughtfully.
The kids all guess — both shake and feel
Each one beneath the tree.

On Christmas morn, the tree stands tall
With pride, as if to say,
"Come and gather 'round me now.
It's finally Christmas Day."

As if we hear, each one obeys,
And families join in love.
The gifts unwrapped and hugs exchanged,
Some even praise the One above.

Then with Christmas over,
It's time to take tree down.
Lights and ornaments are put away
And it lies there, dry and brown.

Memories so beautiful
Linger in each mind,
But take a moment to think about
A Tree where one can find…

A greater Gift that won't wear out
Nor ever need replaced.
This Tree is one of long ago.
On it our sins erased.

The Tree was neither brilliant
Nor grand in any way,
But He who hung upon this Tree
Is the Life, the Truth, the Way.

No lights were strung upon this Tree,
And yet it glowed so bright,
For He who took our place there
Was for the world a Light.

He lived in humble servanthood
For more than thirty years,
And then He died the same way . . .
To take away all fears.

His lifeless form was lifted down
Then put into a tomb,
But even death could not defeat,
And Life breathed from earth's womb.

Heaven broke forth to give a Gift
To every one of us.
It is the greatest Gift of all.
It comes with a name — Jesus!

And every time I decorate
And gaze upon my tree
I think of the cross and Who hung there
And what He's done for me.

All can have this greatest Gift
And never be alone.
He'll fill with His undying love
Your very heart and home.

So, ponder this at Christmastime
As you pick out your tree —
What alone brings peace and joy?
Yes, Jesus. He's the key!

~ 11 ~

Let's Make This a Banner Year!

Lydia E. Harris

*May we shout for joy over your victory
and lift up our banners in the name of our God.*
Psalm 20:5 NIV

Look! The Christmas banners are still up," I told my husband as we drove through a nearby small town. Although the banners must had flapped in the wind for weeks, I noticed them for the first time in January.

"They're so colorful." I commented on each symbol as we drove by: candles, snowflakes, a snowman, a Christmas tree, and gifts. The pattern repeated itself several times as we passed through the town.

After a few moments I asked, "Where's the banner for Jesus?" Why had Christ been left out of Christmas?

Before long I realized that Jesus doesn't need a banner on the street. He wants to be displayed in my life.

The next day, as I drove through the same town again, I deliberately looked up at the banners with a new perspective. How could I be a banner for Jesus and show His love to others? I found plenty of opportunities.

- Apologize to my husband for my unrealistic expectations.
- Smile and say thank you to a fast-food clerk.
- Share my last two favorite Christmas cookies with a neighbor who also loves them.
- Deliver her favorite pudding — tapioca — to a shut-in.
- Send an encouraging note to a relative.
- Pray for those I pass while driving down the street.

Although the city would soon take down its Christmas banners, I realized we can lift up our personal banners in the name of the Lord all year long.

Let's make it a banner year for Jesus!

Let your light shine before others,
that they may see your good deeds
and glorify your Father in heaven.
Matthew 5:16 NIV

~ 12 ~

The Joy of an Unexpected Gift

Lorilyn Roberts

*Are not two sparrows sold for a copper coin?
And not one of them falls to the ground apart from your Father's will.*
Matthew 10:29 NKJV

Arms full of gifts, I stood in line at Wild Birds Unlimited. I was exhausted but satisfied to have finished all my Christmas shopping. I anticipated how excited my daughters would be opening their presents Christmas morning.

As I waited to pay, I noticed hanging on the store rack blue, green and yellow earrings framed into a bird. I leaned over to examine them. How much did they cost?

I looked down at my purchases knowing I'd probably spent too much money. Surely, though, I could indulge myself with some earrings. They would be perfect for me, a bird lover. I added them to my gifts as the cashier rang up my purchases.

When I saw the total, however, I realized I'd exceeded my budget and needed to put something back. I examined everything. What could I return?

I resigned myself to what I needed to do. "Can you take these earrings off the total?" I asked. "I've spent too much money."

The cashier smiled, no doubt appreciating my sadness that I couldn't afford them.

As I left the store, I forgot about the earrings. I was excited about the presents I'd bought for my daughters. The joy of Christmas overtook me as I remembered Christmas morning when I was little — the laughter, the fun, and the excitement.

As usual, Christmas morning arrived too early. Even for teenage daughters, Christmas still held that sense of anticipation when all unwritten rules could be broken. It was the one day they had permission to wake me up and drag me out of bed. Of course, I didn't want to miss any of it.

I couldn't wait to see the joy in their eyes as they opened their gifts. I knew soon they would be out of the house and on their own. College was on the horizon for my oldest one. Careers and perhaps husbands, children, and families would soon follow. I wanted to revel in the spirit of Christmas as long as possible — to make memories that I would remember even into my old age.

As I was sipping my coffee, my younger daughter, Joy, handed me her present to me. "Here," she said.

With delight, I took the wrapped gift and placed it in my lap. When I opened the box, I couldn't believe what I saw. To my amazement, in the box were the earrings I had so longingly put back on the store rack.

I told Joy the story of the earrings. Of all the things she could have bought me as a Christmas gift — or was God the one who gave them to me? Do miracles like that really happen? How do we explain the unexplainable?

When we are young, we don't realize how quickly Father

Time creeps up on us. But it comes to all, even the unsuspecting. Making joyful memories is the best gift Father time gives us — especially on Christmas.

I don't know how many times I've shared the story when someone complimented me on the earrings. Each time I tell the story, I'm reminded God knows exactly what we need in His perfect timing. He even knows the things we don't need, but because He loves us, He gives us those things, too. His desire to bring us joy is unfathomable, even down to the minutest detail — including a pair of earrings in the likeness of a sparrow on Christmas morning.

~ 13 ~

It's Curtains for This Angel!

Annmarie B. Tait

When I was nine years old I only had one wish for Christmas. It wasn't big and it wasn't expensive. It didn't even call for the grand magic of Santa. More than anything, I wanted to wear a costume in our annual grade school Christmas play.

A seemingly simple wish indeed, except for the one problem that wielded significant wish-squelching power. The mere thought of creating a costume launched my mom at break neck speed into absolute delirium. The extent of Mom's talent with a needle and thread culminated in stitching together the unmentionable end of a turkey once stuffed. The end.

Mom devoted herself to convincing me that I'd steal the show as a costume-less narrator. Even at the tender age of nine I found this hard to believe. Let's face it; the play features the Savior of the World. Nice try Mom, but even I'm not that naive.

I forged ahead without worry. I had confidence that if I could just talk God into getting me that role as an angel, He would also provide the costume.

When casting day arrived Sister James Maureen made her rounds up and down the aisles picking and choosing. As she approached me, I pitched my final attempt to cut a deal with God.

While knee deep in negotiating with God, I completely lost track of Sister James Maureen. But, even with my eyes glued shut, I felt her squeaky-clean presence. Either that or someone dropped a giant bar of Ivory Soap right next to my desk.

Slowly, I pried open my eyes and saw her smiling down at me. Holding my angelic fate in her hands, and barely taking a breath she said, "Annmarie, how would you like to be an angel?"

I did not flinch, or bat an eyelash.

"Yes Sister," I replied. "That would be fine."

My composure held fast thanks to the paralysis that had set in while maintaining my perfect posture pose meant to impress the heck out of God. Ah, but what it felt like on the inside! Deep in my heart I turned cartwheels, rang bells, and shouted to the top of my lungs! *I did it! I'm an Angel!*

Every day at practice I paraded around among the largest congregation of angels and shepherds this side of Bethlehem. I still needed a costume, and I prayed like crazy for yet another miracle. After all, I figured if God had brought me this far He had no intention of having me appear on stage naked.

All the while apoplexy loomed closer for my mother.

On the morning of the play, I threw my covers aside and jumped out of bed fully expecting to see an elegant angel costume waiting for me in my closet, complements of God. How disappointing to discover an empty space where I anticipated finding yards of organdy and lace.

I don't think Mom paid much attention until the word "costume" made a beeline from my lips to her ears.

"Sorry Mom" I whined.

She said nothing, but shot me the "glare" with the precision and skill of a Marine Corps marksman. Without uttering one syllable, the words "Are you kidding?" penetrated loud and clear.

"Really Mom. I need an angel costume. Fast!"

"I know I must not have heard you correctly," Mom gasped as she tightened her grip on the rapidly fading hope that I, the darling child would never recklessly hang her out to dry on the clothes line of Mommy mortification making her a perfect point-and-snicker target for all the costume-couture Mommies to ridicule. But, in her mind this is exactly what I'd done. I took my best shot and repeated the plea with a whimper.

"Please, Mom. Won't you *please* make me an angel"?

Those words propelled past all the tension and landed dead center on the pity zone of my mother's heart.

"I suppose we'll have to think of something!" she said.

I had no idea how, but I knew with absolute certainty that if my mother said she would make me look like an angel, somehow she would.

Mom stood in the corner of the kitchen ironing the freshly washed living room curtains waiting for inspiration as the heavenly scent of fabric softener wafted through the air. A shimmering white fabric, loaded with ruffles lent these curtains quite an angelic appearance from where I was standing. Simultaneously we exchanged glances and one stroke of brilliance later, an angel was born.

Operating at full throttle, Mom set to work with a box of straight pins and the living room curtains. She wrapped, pinned, folded, tucked, bedecked and bedazzled me using every scrap of fabric, including the tiebacks, for a sash.

Then I whipped up wings using two wire coat hangers, and a wad of heavy-duty aluminum foil.

Mom rigged the shiny foil wings to my back with enough fishing line to haul in a blue marlin. Tight as a tourniquet it twisted around the wings, under my arms, and over my shoulders in an intricate figure eight pattern that flawlessly cut off all but a trickle of blood circulating through my arms.

When Mom finished, I resembled a left-over float from the Thanksgiving Day Parade. I pirouetted over to the full-length mirror and admired myself. Twirling around on my tiptoes, inflated the voluminous ruffled skirt. What a sight!

There I stood before my mother absolutely ecstatic, with two wire coat hangers boring a hole in my back, numb arms, blue fingers and an entire box of straight pins stabbing me every time I took a breath. Perfection at last!

Our cast of characters included: Mary, Joseph, the innkeeper, three Wise Men, one narrator, forty Angels, and fifteen shepherds. What a crowd!

On stage, the shepherd population cut back significantly on available angel space. Some of the angels complained about not getting to stand up front. Not me. My costume emphasized visibility. You couldn't miss me, even if Sister James Maureen had placed me somewhere near the Equator.

As the angels floated onto the stage a noticeable hush fell over the auditorium. I smiled certain that my heavenly, angelic, heavily-ruffled appearance inspired this reverent response. Most likely the audience didn't know where to look for fear they would burst out laughing at the sight of a child obviously draped in someone's living room curtains.

Without a doubt, an angel graced our presence that day. She sat in the third row back, the fourth seat in from the aisle. With a smile that beamed, *this* angel took as much pride in concocting that costume as I took in wearing it.

Only God could create a mother who could fashion an angel out of a box of straight pins, and the living room curtains. How lucky I am that He gave that mother to me. Some angels come wrapped in an apron, and wearing sensible shoes.

~ 14 ~
A Hole Full of Blessings

Judith Martin Harman

"Whew! I am finally finished!"

I sigh with pleasure as I pop a candy cane into the last of the knitted stockings suitable for Sasquatch. There are eleven now hanging from the mantel and stair railing, one for each of our family and friends who will join us for Christmas morning in a few hours.

A quick mental checklist suggests I can go to bed now. Last-minute gifts are wrapped and under the tree, leftovers from our Christmas Eve gathering are stored for future grazing, stockings are filled, and the sausage-and-egg casserole is overnighting in the fridge. Everything is ready for tomorrow.

"Uh-oh. For *today*," I note, glancing at the clock. "I need to go to bed."

Good sense does not abound when it's two o'clock in the morning, especially at Christmas. I choose to stretch out on the couch for a few minutes as peace and quiet enfold me.

The tiny white lights on the tree, along with the glow from a few stubborn coals in the fireplace, lend a soft contrast to the otherwise dark house. I roll onto my side and stare at the crimson embers. The sense of expectancy that is such a part of Christmas seems to permeate even the coals. They lie smoldering on the grate, alive and pulsating as if they, too, are waiting, hoping for one more chance to burst into glorious flame, if only given a little more kindling or another log.

I suddenly shiver despite the warmth of the remaining embers as I remember a former Christmas. How different things would have been tonight if God had not intervened on a similar cold evening ten years ago!

*****

Mmm! It even smells like Christmas, I thought with excitement as I returned the lid to a pot of simmering chili beans and checked the timer on the oven full of gingerbread. Looking around the cheery kitchen now bedecked with the yard's generous offering of boxwood, pine clippings, and bright red nandina berries, I smiled with gratefulness for this first Christmas in my own house.

My husband, Jim, and I were still enjoying the "firsts" of life in our new home, *new* more accurately describing the owners than the drafty seventy-five-year-old fixer-upper. Actually, *uninhabitable* was the term the bank had used when they refused to give us a loan to buy it. A tragic fire in an upstairs bedroom had left the previous family without a mother and any desire to continue living here. It sat unoccupied for several years, before our "fixing up" had finally made it the place I'd be happy to spend the rest of my life.

"Jim should be home soon," I announced to Charmin, our "squeezably soft" gray tabby. "Let's get everything ready."

I chose a Firestone Christmas album from the stereo cabinet

to set the mood, then made my rounds, tightening the bulb in each window candle and plugging in the extension cord that brought the white pine beside the fireplace to life with hundreds of mini lights, instantly transforming the ceiling into a kaleidoscope of muted rainbow colors.

"It looks beautiful, if I do say so myself," I said, and returned to the kitchen to set the table for six. I was looking forward to our parents joining Jim and me that evening for our first holiday dinner on Roselawn Road.

As the last spoon was placed, the front door flew open, ushering in a blast of chilly air and a cheery greeting. It was my husband, and from the sound of it, his day must have gone well.

"Hey," I said, going to meet him. "How was your day?"

He straightened up from adding a present to the growing pile under the tree and turned to face me, his hazel eyes all but hidden behind cheeks that split to make room for the grin on his face.

"Well, if it isn't the Cheshire Cat! What are you up to?"

"Just did a little shopping today," he answered, trying unsuccessfully to be nonchalant.

"Oh?"

"You're not getting it out of me," he said firmly.

"I'm not planning on trying. You know I want to be surprised," I said, remembering times he had given away his secret because the excitement over his purchase had left him powerless to control his chatter about it. I loved this man's enthusiasm, and still loved to tease him about it.

"Oooh! You're getting better!" I laughed, kissing his cold cheek. "Hey, I was wondering, since our folks are coming for dinner tonight, do you think we could build a fire in the fireplace?"

"Do we have any wood?"

"No, I didn't think about that."

"Maybe we can use part of the limb that fell off the elm tree. It's dead wood, so it should burn well," he said, putting his coat back on and opening the door.

"Oh, thank you, thank you!" I crowed, clapping my hands.

Christmas in our new home, our family coming for dinner, and now a real crackling, smelly-good fire for the first time in our fireplace! My Sweet Baby James was to the rescue again.

I glanced out the window, trying to spot Jim in the gathering dusk, but the Artist who had painted the morning sky with breath-taking shades of pink and orange must have traded his watercolor box for a No. 2 pencil this afternoon. Squinting through the murky grayness, I could see little past the boxwoods lining the driveway.

"I'd better put the flood lights on for him," I said to Charmin. "I don't know how he can see what he's doing."

The timer began to buzz, although my nose had already been directing me to the kitchen. The spicy aroma of tonight's dessert was not about to be limited to the confines of an oven. I wondered what was taking Jim so long as I put the hot pans on a rack to cool.

Charmin and I both jumped when the front door burst open and Jim stumbled in, empty handed, but well decorated with bits of leaves, pine needles, and dirt. This time his eyes were hidden by a grimace of pain.

"What happened?" I asked with alarm.

"I stepped in a hole," he said through clenched teeth.

"What?"

"The ground gave way when I took a step, and down I went. Must have been where one of the underground springs has weakened the surface."

"Are you alright?"

"I think I broke my ankle," he said, hobbling to the sofa.

"Can you get that shoe off?"

I gently tugged at the black-tasseled loafer and rolled down the sock. It looked like a golf ball had slipped under the skin where an old football injury had left his ankle weakened.

"Oh, Honey, I'm so sorry. Can you move it? Do you really think it's broken?"

"Umm, it might just be a sprain," he moaned. "Can you get me some ice to put on it? Sorry, but there's not going to be any fire tonight," he added, as I headed for the kitchen.

"That's okay. Don't worry about it. I'm just sorry you hurt yourself. Thank you for trying," I said, meaning it, but ashamed that I was disappointed about such a trivial thing.

"You know," he said, "Maybe we ought to have a chimney sweep come and check out the fireplace before we use it for the first time anyway. Hard to tell how long it's been since that was done. I'll call someone tomorrow."

Jim's ankle was better in a few days, and as happens when life is busy and time demotes what once seemed urgent, *tomorrow* turned into February before the call was eventually made. The chimney sweep who came, however, didn't take long to give us his assessment — a report that left us stunned.

"Man, you're lucky," he said. "With so many places in the flu where there is no mortar, you'd have gotten fire inside the walls of your house, sure as shootin'. It could have smoldered for days, or gone up overnight as dry as this old place is."

Jim and I looked at each other without blinking.

"It's in bad shape," the man continued, shaking his head. "It's a mighty good thing you never tried to build a fire in there. A mighty good thing."

* * * * *

"A mighty good thing, indeed!" I whisper, still remembering the awful fear that enveloped Jim and me that day as we realized how close we had come to repeating history in this house. Even now, it's hard to think about the previous owners who were not spared tragic loss from a fire when they lived here, yet we were kept safe . . . spared by a hole, of all things.

Over the years, the ground never caved in again, not with Jim or with anybody else. It only happened once, only on the night I had wanted to build a fire, but had no wood.

I stare at the dying embers, marveling at God's goodness.

"Oh, Lord, I'll never understand why you preserved our family and home that night. I didn't even acknowledge that you existed when we bought this house and spent that first Christmas celebrating. — Celebrating ourselves. Our traditions. Our family. Our "good fortune."

Yet in your mercy, you were watching over us, your hand of protection on us. I couldn't have cared less about Jesus — baby in the manger or otherwise — yet by your grace, you slowly led me to Him, and gave me a heart to believe. Here I am, alive, well, and celebrating something truly wonderful — You and your precious love-gift, my Savior."

My heart is full of wonder as I yawn and rise from the couch to begin the nighttime ritual that will be reversed in only a few hours. I turn off the tape player, set the thermostat at sixty-five, and close the fireplace screen, pausing at the nativity scene to upright a fallen camel and remove a sheep from the roof of the stable, wondering what version of the Christmas Story the children were telling this time. Unplugging the last string of lights, my eyes slowly adjust to the darkness, then quickly fill with the tears I've been holding back.

"Oh, Jesus, you left all the glories of heaven to live in this world of sorrow and become one of us, to live the perfect life I never could live, to die the horrible death I deserve for all my sins, and now, there You are in heaven, still helping me, praying for me, preparing my forever-home, and waiting for me to join You. Thank you.

"Lord, I know you preserved my life, not only for a few fleeting years on Roselawn Road, but for all eternity. May I never, never stop thanking you."

Tiptoeing up the stairs, I feel close to bursting with gratefulness. The new day has yet to dawn, but contrary to what my tears suggest, I am already having a very, merry Christmas. I am simply remembering, and rejoicing once more in God's marvelous gifts to me . . . even a certain hole which appeared in our yard so many winters ago. A hole full of blessings, for sure.

~ 15 ~
The Gift of Christmas Visitors

Jan Elder

My nonagenarian mother, Eleanor, needed more help than I could give. After eleven days in the hospital, she was transferred to a nursing home affiliated with the senior community she'd lived in for many years. Although now wheelchair bound, Mom was still mentally alert. While the long-term care facility was a good one and took great care of her physically, the staff didn't have the time to attend to my mother's mental, spiritual, or emotional needs.

And Christmas was just around the corner, the season in which a flurry of holiday activity commenced. After making the fifty-mile trip to see Mom nearly every day for four months, I was dog-tired from carrying the load all alone. How could I make this very special season of the year a joyful time for my mother without wearing myself to a frazzle?

I prayed about it, asked God to provide wisdom as to what to do. That's when divine inspiration popped into my head, the notion to call Pastor Kelly, the compassionate associate minister at Mom's church. That wonderful, resourceful woman knew just what to do. She called in the troops, so to speak, and word got out that Mom needed visitors.

Pastor Kelly whipped up a spreadsheet and even included a notice in the weekly bulletin. Mom had attended the same church for over fifty years, and there were many people willing and eager to assist. Slots began to fill up, and visitors arrived to spread some comfort and make the season shiny and bright.

Songs were sung, stories read, conversations hummed, and hands were held. People — friends and family alike — brought in or mailed scads of Christmas cards. Love blossomed as I tacked them all around the walls of her room. Gifts arrived, both handmade and store bought, chosen with care. She treasured a teddy bear my cousin, Judy, brought and often held the squishy animal in her arms. A bouquet of gorgeous roses arrived to scent the air with sweetness, a thoughtful gift from my cousin, Nancy. A pair of silly, soft reindeer antlers appeared; my mother laughingly wore them with pride on Christmas day.

My gratefulness abounded at everyone's thoughtfulness. Pastor Kelly reminded me that my mother was reaping the rewards of the seeds of kindness she'd sown over the many decades. Galatians 6:9 tells us: *"Let us not become weary in doing good, for at the proper time we will reap a harvest if we do not give up."*

As I was growing up, my mother gave of her time, her energy, and her finances more times than I can count. She was a true prayer warrior who sent up thousands of prayers, praises, and petitions. That was just Mom, an example of how to live.

In a similar way, each of those precious people doubtless had no idea of the special gift they were bestowing on both of us. The experience changed me, showed me a better way to live, the satisfaction it gives to seek out even small ways to make a difference in the lives of those around me.

When Mom passed away at the age of ninety-five, her guest book showed hundreds of signatures. Each person who walked into her room reflected the goodness of God. Now, when I wake up, I pray "Jesus, open my eyes and show me how I can be a blessing to someone today."

Even a small act of kindness can change the world, one person at a time. It did for my mom and me.

~ 16 ~

Glory Be

Dee Bowlin

When I was a child growing up in Wisconsin, my parents took my sister and me to the Lutheran Church in Hales Corners to attend the Christmas Eve service. The frigid Wisconsin winters meant bundling up in coats, scarves, and mittens to hurry into the warm, candle-lit sanctuary to find a seat before the pews were full.

When the service ended, Mom and Dad would guide us to the front door, where the minister shook my hand or gave me a holiday hug. Then we stepped outside to witness even more magic of the season. A gentle snowfall sparkled in the night sky, covering the ground with a soft blanket and caressing our faces as we walked down the church steps and to the parking lot. It was never a blizzard or paralyzing snowfall. Without a wind to blow the snow into drifts, it calmly fell upon our shoulders to greet the holiday as we headed home to get ready for Santa Claus and family feasts on Christmas Day.

It seemed to me it always snowed on Christmas Eve. I looked forward to this heavenly gift every year.

When I left Wisconsin and moved to Oklahoma to attend college, I rarely saw snow on Christmas. Now that I live in

Roanoke, Virginia, I admit I pray for snow while I am in church on Christmas Eve.

I learned Christmas carols in my Sunday School classes, so I could sing along with the choir and congregation to rejoice in the birth of Christ. Throughout the years, whether I attend church alone or go with a friend to their church for the holiday, the songs of the season still fill my heart, with or without snow.

I wanted to write a Christmas song of my own, and when I learned of a poetry form known as a "Samisen," the rhythm, rhyme scheme, and repetition provided the platform I was looking for. This charming old form was created as a song lyric to be sung to a shamisen or samisen, which is a three-string Japanese instrument.

My song, "Glory Be," is written for the young or young at heart. I composed a simple melody to go with the words so my friends can sing it to their children.

Glory Be

There's a bright star in the heavens — Glory Be.
    Glory Be.
Over Bethlehem, they tell us — Glory Be.
        Will it lead us to the cradle
        of a King for you and me?
        All the angels are rejoicing,
        so let's follow them and see.
        Glory Be.

There's a baby in the manger — Glory Be.
    Glory Be.
In the arms of Virgin Mary — Glory Be.
        He was born here in the stable
        with the oxen and the sheep,
        but His love shines so divinely
        as He lies here fast asleep.
        Glory Be.

There are Wise Men bringing presents — Glory Be.
    Glory Be.
And they're kneeling down before Him — Glory Be.
        We have found our Lord and Savior
        in the Star's bright guiding light
        and the singing of the angels
        on this holy Christmas night.
        Glory Be.

~ 17 ~
Making Space for Christmas

J.J. LeVan

"There's almost eighty of us if everybody shows up," my brother said, standing in the middle of their freshly finished great room. "I think we can squeeze us in for Christmas. Yeah, I think we'll all fit in here." His face was beaming.

The beautiful vaulted ceiling, ample natural light, and shiplap walls were enough to make Chip and Joanna Gaines proud. It was perfect.

"I think it's amazing," I tried to sound reassuring, but my face must have conveyed the dread in my heart.

Christmas can be hard for us. My autistic adult son usually starts playing his favorite Christmas music in mid-September on a loop, but he isn't a fan of large Christmas gatherings, especially groups with squealy children (and oh boy, do we have a lot of them!)

The noise, the presents, the bustling of festive people — all of it is a recipe for emotional meltdowns for those on the autism spectrum. In fact, just the year before, he completely opted out of going to our Christmas party at our family farm. My unreliable communicator knew it would be too overstimulating and too much, even if it was the most wonderful time of the year for him.

He found enough words to let us know how he felt and simply said, "No party."

I had prayed for years that my son would be able to communicate words that told us his thoughts. It had taken thirty-one years, but we were thrilled for his self-advocacy.

As thankful as I was for the language, his message left a papercut on my mom heart.

My sister-in-law sensed my concern and chimed into the conversation. "What can we do to help Blake have a good time?"

A lump swelled in my throat. *How kind of her.* The party was weeks away, but she was determined to serve and make room to include my big guy's sure-to-be-overwhelmed heart in the midst of our wild horde.

"Christmas is just so loud and crazy for him. He might just need a place to escape to be able to get through the day," I said. Before I left, they promised to figure something out for him.

On the day of the gathering, we piled into the car with our twenty pounds of steaming mashed potatoes, crockpot full of gravy, and our snarky white elephant gifts. I believe it was about the moment I was feeling profoundly thankful that we were on time that my car began sputtering and lunging.

When we pulled into the grass at the side of the road, we were so close to my brother's house that I could almost smell the turkey. We passed off our potatoes through the passenger window to my new nephew-in-law who stopped by in his giant work truck.

My husband (bless his heart) had just decided to stay put and wait on the tow truck rescue, when my daughter and son-in-law rolled up just moments after the herky-jerky halt. I coaxed my son into their car and we headed to the celebration together, leaving my husband in the cold.

All of these unexpected disruptions were not listed on my son's pocket planner schedule. He started to feel unsettled as we crawled out of the tiny back seat of our kid's Honda Civic. With a deep breath, we gathered our presents together, and walked up to the door that would unlock the rest of our day.

One twist of the doorknob unleashed the merry mayhem.

Happy children swirled around our knees as wonderful whiffs of ham and turkey filled the air. The roar of holly jolly conversation was everywhere. It was a perfect family Christmas for almost everyone — but Blake. I took one look at him and knew it was going to be a challenging day for him.

My sister-in-law's face poked through the crowd. "Hey, come here. Bring Blake."

Navigating us through the jungle of cousins, she led us up the stairway to their bedroom. There was a Scotch-taped sign on the door in simple pen and paper that read, "Blake's Quiet Place."

As my son read the words aloud, she opened the door and led us into their beautiful bedroom that all but silenced the others downstairs. The TV was already parked on my son's favorite YouTube channel. He could scroll through as many Sesame Street, Muppets, and Wheel of Fortune reruns as his heart desired.

"I told the other kids that *this* is *Blake's Space* and it isn't for them today," she said to Blake. I turned to look at my quiet man standing beside me, who was keenly attentive to what was happening.

"It's perfect," he said. His face held a glow of appreciation.

We made our way downstairs just in time for the prayer before dinner. He made it through the food line, which included some gorgeous gluten-free holiday recipes for him and the GF others. He made it through the great hall dining experience by sitting with his brother and surrounding cousins. He even almost made it through the reading of the Luke 2 Christmas Story, but had to tap out before "there was no room in the inn."

He could go no further emotionally. His heart was overwhelmed, but he knew that someone who loved him had a place prepared for him.

After the opening of the presents, I took a peek upstairs to see how he was doing. To my surprise, his little toe-headed, curly-haired cousin — who had just received his own autism diagnosis — had also squirreled away from the crowd and taken refuge in that haven.

Loved, understood, and included, the two took a much-needed, silent break from the day. Happy as clams, they were able to celebrate the season in their own special way.

Glory to God in the highest, and on earth peace, goodwill toward men, indeed, my heart whispered in praise, as I shut the door. Even though my son had skipped the gift exchange downstairs, "Blake's Quiet Place" was the best gift we received that year.

My big brother was right. Their Christmas held plenty of room for *everyone*.

~ 18 ~

Sweet Happy

Sharilynn Hunt

Christmas. Just the thought of it stirs up my childhood memories of fruit cakes, candy, decorated cookies, and my grandmother, Nona's, caramel popcorn balls. She came from Pennsylvania with a lineage of traditional German cooks who referred to their homeland as "Deutschland" or "Dutch." One of her old Pennsylvania Dutch cookbooks included caramel in many of its sweet recipes. As a child, I looked forward to biting into my own popcorn ball every Christmas Day amid all the other cousins and members of her large family.

When I was a young stay-at-home mom, I worked one day a week for my friend, Grace, in her Italian food store. One Christmas season, she handed me a bag and said, "I made my homemade caramel popcorn for you and the family. I call it Karmel Korn."

I opened the bag for a bite. "Oh, my!" I exclaimed. "This popcorn melts in my mouth! Grace, I know the kids will love it. Will you share the recipe with me?"

The following weekend, I made a batch for my husband and two children. An afternoon of labor disappeared in one short evening. "Hey, do you guys realize how long it took me to fix this snack?" I asked. They nodded and smiled with their hands still moving from bowls to mouths.

Like my own grandmother, I started the tradition of making this tasty caramel treat during the holidays for my family. We enjoyed it, but I never made a large enough quantity to give any away. Then, years later, I began sharing the love.

At the beginning of each Christmas season, I pull out Grace's treasured, faded, handwritten recipe. She passed away years ago, but she would be honored to know that her edible legacy found many homes.

The cooking process has become a team effort with my husband, David, helping me. Because we found that microwave popcorn does not absorb the caramel well, he pops the corn by hand. Standing over the stove, he uses our "whirly" pot, which keeps the lid closed while he flips the pot upside down and right side up over the heat. No kernel is left behind. Meanwhile, I get out my Dutch oven pot and remember with nostalgia my short, white-haired Nona cooking over her stove for her family.

Over the years, I've tweaked Grace's ingredients by melting real butter (not margarine) with honey (not corn syrup), stirring the mixture until it boils. Then, I add five more minutes of mixing time. When I remove the pot from the heat, I feel like a chemist as I stir in the vanilla and baking soda. The hot mixture bubbles up like a liquid volcano ready to blow. Thankfully, no explosions ever occurred in my kitchen!

After pouring the scalding liquid over the popped corn in large, greased pans, the baking process begins. The oven becomes an incubator ready to hatch this tasty delight. Every fifteen minutes, we turn the mixture over in the caramel sauce.

When it's finished baking, my husband spreads the hot popcorn onto cookie sheets to cool, moving them around so they will not clump together. Then, we repeat the entire process. Pans and cookie sheets cover the counters, and the kitchen smells like a candy factory. When we're finished, we cannot sample another bite of this yummy treat.

In addition to giving it to our family on Christmas Day, we now allow time to make larger quantities for others. One season, we gave away a total of thirty-two quarts of Karmel Korn to neighbors and friends. People carry their bags away with thankful comments and big smiles. Those who are of a certain age mention their memories of munching on the caramel corn found in the famous Cracker Jack boxes when they were young; store-bought kettle or caramel corn was not readily available as it is today.

In the fall, people asked, "Will you be making that delicious popcorn again this year?"

Once, a friend offered to share her bag with her mother on Christmas Eve. Unfortunately, there was little left to share. So, we began sending two bags of "sweet happy" to satisfy their holiday munchies.

In our fast-paced world, we enjoy giving and receiving gifts during the holidays. It blesses us to share our Karmel Korn with others, yet it's soon gone, and not everyone can enjoy its sweet flavor. Christmas reminds us that God shared the sweetest gift of all, Jesus Christ . . . who offers eternal life for us all. The true Sweet Happy.

Karmel Korn

Ingredients

1 cup butter

2 cups of brown sugar (I mix half dark and light)

½ cup of honey (I use local honey)

1 tsp. of salt

½ tsp. baking soda

1 tsp. vanilla

6 quarts of premium popped corn

Instructions

Melt butter and stir in brown sugar, honey, and salt. Bring to a boil, stirring constantly. Boil for an additional 5 minutes, stirring continuously. Remove from heat; add soda and vanilla. Pour the mixture over the popcorn, covering it well. Turn into two large (9 x13 inch) pans. Bake 1 hour at 250°. Turn the kernels every 15 minutes. Remove, cool, and break apart.

~ 19 ~

Kiss the Cook

Connie K. Pombo

"How are we ever going to buy Christmas gifts this year?" I asked with tears in my eyes.

Mark, my husband of ten years, cupped my face in his hands and silently mouthed the words, "We're not."

It was our first Christmas back in the States after spending six years in Italy where our older son was born. We returned just in time for our second son to be born in Walnut Creek, California. Afterward, our little family settled in Brentwood and rented from my parents. We lived on a pauper's income that year — $900 a month, which had to cover rent, health insurance, food, gas, and utilities.

I planted zucchini in the back yard. After three months, we had what we called "zucchini world." Zucchini bread, zucchini soup, and zucchini pasta for three "square" meals a day. Mark rode his bike to work, and I homeschooled our older son, Jeremy, so we only needed to use the car for shopping and going to church.

It would be a slim Christmas, and I was overwhelmed with things to do. Mark's family celebrated Christmas in a big way. There were so many gifts under the tree that they spilled out into the entryway and dining room. My family was more modest with gift-giving; it wasn't a priority.

After ten years of marriage, I had come to dislike Christmas because it was always the same story. "What are we going to buy your family for Christmas?" I'd ask. It was stressful to worry about stretching our budget to accommodate their kind of Christmas.

That night, after I got the boys to bed, I went through all my cross-stitch material and found the perfect pattern. There were two hearts, one on each side, with the words "Kiss the Cook" in the middle. It could be framed in an embroidery hoop with a ruffle made from material or lace. I would need to make ten hoops in all. It was already the middle of October, so I had a little over two months to complete the task. Thankfully, I had enough fabric in my stash to match the colors in everyone's kitchen. And, of course, I'd make zucchini bread to go along with it.

The only time I had to work on the gifts was after the boys went to bed. I made sure everything was done during the day, including lesson plans for Jeremy, dishes washed, and laundry folded and put away. If I worked a few hours every night, I'd have them finished by Christmas.

What I hadn't planned on was both boys getting sick with earaches and strep throat, which meant doctor visits and medicine. When one got better, the other one got worse. It was a vicious cycle. At three o'clock one Saturday morning in late November, I realized that the "Kiss the Cook" project might have to be abandoned, and zucchini bread might have to suffice. I knew my family wouldn't mind, but Mark's family was a different story. I simply couldn't arrive empty handed on Christmas Eve for the big Italian tradition of eating dinner, opening gifts, and attending Mass.

I persevered even though I barely slept during the week leading up to Christmas. On the eve of Christmas Eve, I stayed up all night to finish up the ruffles that adorned each hoop, wrap them in boxes, and add zucchini bread in red and green bags.

As Mark loaded up the "sleigh" with the kids and gifts, I made sure that I had extra zucchini bread — with the recipe written on the front — just in case I had forgotten someone. The drive across the Bay Bridge to Mark's childhood home in San Mateo was bumper-to-bumper. But all was forgotten when we pulled into the driveway and smelled the makings of a Pombo Family Christmas. It was all fish, of course, starting with shrimp cocktail, oysters on the half shell, crab cioppino soup, crab and prawns. Mark's mom made sure she put in her order at Petrini's Italian Market months in advance to ensure everything was the very best.

When I saw all the gifts under the tree and spilling into the entryway, I started to panic. What if my best wasn't good enough? Maybe we could leave right after dinner and spare the disappointment on everyone's faces.

Too late.

After dinner, we all gathered in the living room, and the gift-giving began in a time-honored tradition: reading out the name (to and from) and waiting until that person opened the gift and said "thank you" before going on to the next person. It went on for hours. Since I placed our gifts near the wall, away from the tree, maybe ours would be overlooked.

No such luck.

"To Mom and Dad — Love Connie, Mark and Boys!" Dad

Pombo read aloud from the gift tag. Mom Pombo smiled warmly and asked, "What have we here?"

I glanced over at Mark, with my heart racing, and gave him a weak smile as all eyes were on Mom Pombo.

I had wrapped Mom and Dad's gift in the nicest paper I could find and added a handmade card. It was the boys' handprints sprinkled with red and green glitter. And I made Mom's hoop in blue to match her kitchen colors. I grabbed Mark's hand and squeezed tightly as Mom opened the box and peeled away the tissue paper. She clutched her hand over her heart, with tears filling her eyes, as she held up "Kiss the Cook."

"You made this?" she asked tentatively.

I nodded my head and felt a sense of relief wash over me. Mom Pombo got up from her chair, walked across the living room, and kissed me on the cheek. "I know exactly where I'm going to put this," she said, as her face filled with a bright smile. When she got back to her chair, she carefully put "Kiss the Cook" back in the box — as if it was a piece of fine china. My heart swelled as I wiped away the tears. I hardly noticed the stack of cashmere sweaters, pearls, and glass figurines next to her.

Years after that Christmas back in the States — even after we moved to Pennsylvania — I enjoyed coming back to Mom Pombo's kitchen and seeing "Kiss the Cook" over the stove where she attached blue ribbons with a gold fork and spoon on either side. It was the only decoration in her kitchen, and it stayed there for three more decades until we kissed the "cook" goodbye.

~ 20 ~

The Stables

Kay S. Walsh

The entrance to the motel was reminiscent of an old cowboy movie set: two huge concrete stallions painted black with white flowing manes, front hooves reared in the air forming an arch of sorts. As we drove under the figures on a hot July evening, I laughed and whispered to my husband, "Quite an appropriate entrance to a motel named The Stables."

We were returning from a delightful week of vacation with relatives in Ohio. We hoped to make it to our home in Virginia by nightfall; however, exhaustion began to take over as we traveled with our nine-month-old daughter and our three-and-a-half-year-old son. Checking for a simple, clean place to spend the night, our search led us to The Stables Motel in Parkersburg, West Virginia. My husband and I sighed with relief even as we faced the task of unloading the essentials to our first-floor room.

However, our son David had other ideas. He pulled back the curtains and spotted a Holiday Inn just up the hill. Since staying with my parents in a Holiday Inn once, he thought any Holiday Inn was "the bestest!" He was insistent that we needed to pack up and move to the Holliday Inn . . . right then! We explained that this was just a short stopover so we could get some sleep. We would stay where we were.

However, like any child that age, he continued to ask, reframing the question each time in hopes we would change our minds. *Why did we want to stay at The Stables when there was a fun adventure waiting at the top of the hill? Why did we want to go to bed now?*

In his disappointment, he continued to stare out the window at the Holiday Inn, even after the late sunset of a long summer day.

To appease him, we ate breakfast at the Holiday Inn the next morning. He didn't mention our motel "faux pas" again.

We adjusted back to our normal life and by the time snow began to fall, our vacation was a distant memory.

One Sunday morning the following December, David dashed out of his Sunday School class with a big smile. He jumped into my arms, saying, "Guess what, Mom! Guess what!"

"What?"

"I know why we stayed at The Stables!"

In response to my puzzled look, he added, "Remember . . . the motel where we stayed after going to see Aunt Ann!"

After a second of shifting my thoughts back to the summer, I repeated his question, "Why did we stay at The Stables?"

His response?

"Because there was no room at the inn . . . you know, the Holiday Inn!"

Jesus called the children to Him and said, "Let the little children come to Me, and do not hinder them, for the kingdom of God belongs to such as these."
Luke 18:16 NIV

~ 21 ~
The Story of Christmas

David Sowards

King David had descendants, too numerous to name.
One of them was Joseph, who would gain lasting fame.
Joseph was engaged to a woman named Mary.
God said to her one night, "My child, you shall carry."
All that Joseph wanted was to do that which was right.
He considered leaving her, but God appeared to him one night.
The Lord said, "Take Mary to be your lawful wife."
"She will bear my child who will save all with his life."
The emperor Augustus ordered a census taken around.
Every man had to register by going to his hometown.
So Joseph and Mary left to go to Bethlehem.
By now she was expecting, so a donkey aided them.
When they got to the city, there was no room for strangers.
The only place for the baby was in a borrowed manger.
So Jesus was born, wrapped in cloths, and laid in that humble place.
It was a small beginning for the savior of the human race.
While the shepherds of that country were in fields tending flocks,
An angel of the Lord came down and gave them quite a shock!
"Don't be afraid," The angel said. "I bring good news for you."
"On this day, your savior is born, so this is what you should do."
"You will find the child in a manger, wrapped in swaddling clothes."
And then a great army of angels suddenly arose.

The angels sang their praises to the savior born that day.
The shepherds got excited and left right away.
They found the baby, and were quite amazed.
They went back to their fields, full of hope and praise.
Now Bethlehem was in Judea, where Herod ruled as king.
After Jesus was born, some wise men asked him things.
"Where is this baby born who will be king of the Jews?"
"We have seen his star in the east, can you give us any news?"
When Herod learned of their wish to find and worship the child,
He became angry and disturbed and his evil thoughts ran wild.
He consulted withe priests and the teachers of the law.
They studied all their writings and this is what they saw.
"From Bethlehem in Judea, a new leader will reveal
That he is the chosen king of the people of Israel."
Herod sent for the wise men and learned about the star from them.
And when he found where it appeared, he sent them to Bethlehem.
Herod gave them these instructions, "Go see what you can do."
"Try and find this child so I may praise him, too."
So the wise men left, they found the star, and followed it.
It led them to the house of Jesus, where they came to visit.
When they arrived at his house, they saw the child with Mary.
The wise men knelt and worshiped him and gave him gifts they carried.
Gold, frankincense, and myrrh were given from their hands.
Then the wise men left Jesus to return to their own lands.
But they did not go to Herod, because God warned them that day.
In their dreams, he said, "Don't go back!" So they returned another way.
The first Christmas was so very long ago.
Yet it changed the world we now know.

~ 22 ~

The Mrs. Claus Blessing
A Fictional Christmas Tale

By Ane Mulligan

Boxes in various stacks encircled Janet Clausen. Each was filled with Christmas decor and ornaments collected over the years. The smallest was from her childhood — not a lot had managed to survive through the decades. Next to it stood an old blue tub. Gazing at the container made a smile tug at her lips. Ralph had bought that tub after she purchased an overabundance of ornaments, garland, nativities, and Santas for their first Christmas. They'd moved into their house shortly before the holidays. In a frenzy to make their home festive, she had gone a tad overboard.

She sighed, staring at what Ralph laughingly called her "Mrs. Claus" proclivity. Each year, she bought new additions for her collections. And each year, as her family enjoyed the decorations, she received a blessing. So, with her love of everything Christmas, why couldn't she gather the enthusiasm to decorate this year?

She slipped off the reindeer headband as her gaze migrated from the slough of boxes to the wall of family photos. Their children were grown now and busy with their own Christmas preparations. Her heart warmed, thinking about her son and daughter.

Jonathan's wife was the perfect daughter-in-law. After Ralph had graduated to Heaven, Sherry made sure Janet was included in every holiday. Their relationship was close and loving.

Janet ran her finger over the top of one dust-free photo frame. Two years ago, her daughter and son-in-law had moved to New York City for his job. Now, she flew to New York to spend Thanksgiving and have an early Christmas with them.

Christmas day was at Jonathan and Sherry's house. There wasn't anyone to enjoy these decorations but her — and normally, she did. But now, standing amidst the boxes, she wasn't sure why she bothered any longer. It was a lot of work, and nobody spent Christmas at her house.

A light knock on the front door pulled Janet from her musing. When she opened it, two small children occupied her front porch.

She couldn't help smiling at their sweet faces staring up at her. "Well, good afternoon. May I help you?" she asked.

"We moved in next door this morning," the eldest replied.

Janet hadn't paid much attention to the moving van. It wasn't there very long,

"I'm Mattie. I'm eight, and this is Timmy," she pointed to her brother. "He's five. Our baby sister, Susie, is home with Mommy. She's two. Mommy told me to ask if you had any milk to spare for Susie. Mommy's trying to get us unpacked and Susie's bed ready for tonight. The milk we brought from our old apartment got spilled."

Oh, my goodness. "Of course I do. Come on in."

Mattie shook her head. "We can wait here."

Of course. Their mother was raising them right.

"I'll be right back," Janet said, and walked to her kitchen. When she returned with the milk, Timmy was staring into her front room.

"What are all those boxes?" he asked.

"My Christmas decorations." She handed Mattie a half-gallon of milk. "Here you go."

"Thank you."

"You're lucky. We don't have any decorations," Timmy blurted.

Mattie shook her head and shushed him. "You don't tell people that."

"Why not? It's true." He stared up at Janet. "Our daddy went to Heaven last year just before Christmas. He was a soldier."

Oh dear. Those poor babies. Their poor mama. "Do you have a Christmas tree?"

"No, ma'am," Mattie said shaking her head. "Mommy said maybe next year."

The children took the milk home. Janet stood on the porch to watch them safely home. How carefully they crossed the grass to their house. What sweet children.

She went into the kitchen and began to bake cookies. When they were done, she'd take a plate over to welcome their mother to the neighborhood. Maybe a casserole would be good to fortify the children before they had the snickerdoodles. She chose a recipe her children had loved. Hamburger and macaroni with a cheesy topping — what wasn't to love about that?

Humming Christmas carols while she baked, by four o'clock Janet had the casserole and cookies ready. Her kitchen smelled of cinnamon, the result of a good deed. Yet the blessing of it eluded her. What else was needed? "What have I missed, Lord?"

Not receiving an answer, she loaded the offerings into a padded carrier and crossed the lawn to the house next door. A moment after she rang the doorbell, three little faces peeked through the leaded glass.

"Mommy, it's that nice lady from next door," Mattie called out, smiling through the glass.

A minute later, their mother opened the door. She couldn't be more than thirty — if that. Her blond hair was in a cockeyed ponytail, making Janet grin. Her children were clean with their hair nicely combed, but she obviously hadn't paid much attention to herself. Janet liked her immediately.

The woman held out her hand. "Hello. I'm Gracie. Thank you so much for the milk. I wanted to get our beds together and the basic necessities unpacked before I made a trip to the store." She put one arm around her children. "I don't know anyone to babysit yet."

"Well, you don't need to go right now. This," Janet held out the casserole carrier, "is your supper and cookies for dessert, and I'll be glad to bring over a gallon of milk for you before morning. Welcome to the neighborhood."

Gracie's face lit up. "Oh, you are an angel. You have no idea!"

Yes, Janet did. Memories of a move when her husband was on a business trip made her smile. She'd been so harried with her own young ones clamoring for food.

"Won't you come in? Of course, we're mostly boxes."

Janet laughed. "My front room looks the same."

Gracie tilted her head, clearly confused. "Did you just move in too?"

"No, but I was trying to decide whether or not to put up Christmas decorations. I go to my son's house for Christmas, so nobody will be home to enjoy them."

Sorrow crossed Gracie's face, but glancing at her children, she quickly sent it packing. "Would you like some coffee? I unpacked my coffee maker first."

Janet got the feeling her acceptance would mean a lot to Gracie. "I'd like that."

In the kitchen, Gracie put the casserole on the counter and made the coffee. Although Gracie was around the age of Janet's children, a friendship was born that afternoon.

Gracie told her they moved here because she got a decent job, one that would provide for her children. But right now, things were still a little tight. The children would have Christmas presents, but there wasn't enough to add a tree with all the trappings.

That's it! Thank you, Lord.

Gracie's cheerful attitude, surprising after losing her husband last year, impressed Janet. She would love to learn their story, but not yet. It was too soon. So instead, she had Gracie giggling over stories of the shenanigans her own children had pulled — none serious or dangerous. She didn't want Mattie, Timmy, or Susie to get ideas.

At five o'clock, Janet rose. "Gracie, I'm delighted y'all moved in next door. Call me anytime if you need anything." She left her number on a piece of paper on the table.

When she once again stood in her front room gazing at all those boxes, her revelation took shape. She called Jonathan first since he would inherit most of the decorations.

After she told him about the new neighbors and her idea, he chuckled. "Ma, that's so like you. Go right ahead, Mrs. Claus. Just save me the ones from your childhood and your and Dad's first Christmas. Do you need any help?"

Her firstborn had her sensibilities. "Carrying them over, I suspect."

"Sherry is at her book club. The kids and I will come on over."

Delighted to see her grandchildren anytime, Janet emptied her childhood ornaments into the box of her and Ralph's first Christmas and marked it for her son. Then, sorting through all the cartons, she pulled together a collection for Gracie and the kiddos, along with a seven-foot artificial tree. If they wanted a real one, that could come next year.

Her grandchildren were excited to hear about new kids living next door. They especially liked being in on the surprise for them. Janet was proud Jonathan and Sherry were raising their children to have servants' hearts.

They waited until the downstairs lights went out next door, then they carried the tree and boxes over, leaving them on the side porch.

Janet couldn't wait to hear the children's delight when they discovered the surprise. She kissed her grandchildren and son goodnight, thanking them for their help.

Back in her front room, she set up the nativity she and Ralph had bought in Mexico on a vacation many years ago. That and her mother's Christmas tablecloth on the kitchen table were enough Mrs. Claus for this year. Maybe next year . . . she chuckled.

In the morning, delighted squeals and laughter from next door woke her. Janet peeked out the window. The children and Gracie knelt over the boxes. Her new neighbor looked up at Janet's house and smiled.

She hadn't surprised her new friend, but it didn't matter. Janet knew why she'd wasn't enthusiastic about decorating this year. This Christmas was for Gracie and her children. And after all, Janet could always go next door to view the festive decor.

She let the curtain slide back into place, raised her eyes to Heaven, and winked. "Thank you, Lord, for this year's Mrs. Claus blessing. That was a good idea. And please be sure to let Ralph know. I think it will make him smile."

~ 23 ~

Mary's Mom
An Empty Nest Christmas Tale

Karen Cook

I snagged one of the last carts in front of the Kroger's and headed inside. At 6 A.M. I planned to beat the Christmas Eve crowds, but evidently, I wasn't the only one with that idea.

The Christmas music on the speakers played Bing Crosby's "White Christmas" followed by The Waitress' "Christmas Wrapping" — an odd segue I thought. I wove through customers pushing heaping carts on my way over to the meat section. A stock clerk hurriedly emptied a cart of turkeys and roasts into the nearly empty meat case. I spied two lonely rib-eye steaks in the back corner and snatched them up. My next and last stop was in produce to pick up two baking potatoes and a bag of premade salad, then I made my way to the long line for self-check out.

In the self-check kiosk next to me a little blond girl in a red taffeta dress began jumping up and down cheering, "Christmas! Christmas! Christmas baby! We're gonna have a Christmas baby!"

The grey-haired woman next to her stopped scanning items and grabbed the girl firmly by the hand, "Molly, please look at Grandma," the woman said firmly. The girl looked up, frowning.

"I know you're excited about your new baby brother, but we can't be loud in the store, Honey." Molly looked down pondering her grandma's words, then resumed her chant, softly to herself, raising up and down on her tip toes.

Molly's grandma turned to me, "I apologize. My daughter is due any day now. My granddaughter, Molly, is so excited."

"You're fine!" I assured her, "We should all have more of that excitement at Christmas — especially with a new baby coming!"

I smiled and waved at the little girl as I took my receipt and left. A bittersweet twinge struck me remembering how my little Gwen danced around me the same way when I was eight months pregnant with our son David. Gwen would put her face against my swollen belly and whisper, "Merry Christmas, David"

My "little" Gwen grew into a logistic specialist, and quite a good one. Earlier this year a large non-profit offered her a district manager position in Melbourne Australia. At the time we all agreed it wouldn't be worth the two days of flying for her to come home a week for the holidays.

"Mom, we can FaceTime. It won't be the same, but if I call you at 10 P.M. my time on Christmas eve, it will be 8 A.M. Christmas morning for you."

She was right, it was not the same, but it would have to do.

This would be our first Christmas without David as well. This year had been a whirlwind of change for him. He graduated from college in April. In July he married his college sweetheart, a rosy-faced girl named Beth who positively glowed in her pearly gown at the altar with David. David's freshly-earned engineering degree opened the door for a job near Beth's parents' town in

South Dakota, and Beth quickly found a nursing job in a local clinic. Their homestead was settled.

Before Thanksgiving David had sheepishly called me, "Mom, I know we said that we would come back to Michigan for Christmas, but Beth's dad is worried about us making that trip in the winter. I guess it gets real bad out here; more than it does at home. Blizzards can pop up out of nowhere." He took a deep breath, "Mom, Beth and I think we'll just stay here for Christmas . . . at least this year. We'll try to come out for Dad's birthday in April instead . . . . Sorry to do this, I know you were looking forward to having us come."

I struggled to keep my voice steady. "No David, I think it's a wise decision. No sense risking it. I'll be just that much more happy to see you in April."

I could hear him let the air out of his chest. "I'm so sorry Mom, I was looking forward to seeing you, too. And I know Gwen will be gone. Not a great Christmas for you guys.

"It's okay, I said. "You guys have to spread your wings, It's the endgame of parenting — to have successful children live their lives."

"You know, we can FaceTime. It won't be the same, but if we get up early South Dakota time, we can sorta be together at eight on Christmas morning."

I pulled into the garage still thinking Gwen and David's faces on a phone would be so very different from the traditional eight o'clock full-pancake breakfast before church and then gifts.

It would just be James and I this year.

"I'm home!" I announced, setting the bag of groceries on the counter.

"Oh Hi!" James' head peeked around the corner of the big artificial Christmas tree in the front room. "I don't know what happened to these lights, they worked fine last year." James knelt in the middle of tree lights, half of them blinking the other half stubbornly dark.

"I know you'll figure it out. Hey, I grabbed the last two rib-eyes they had. It was a mad house. They were almost out of everything! Do you still want to grill 'em or try that Chinese sauté?"

"Grill. I'm not afraid of standing out in a little snow. Besides, it's our first non-traditional Christmas for two. I think we should do it right."

James rose from the twisted mess. "I give up on these lights. Think I'll go out and see if I can find some cheap ones at Lowes."

"We don't *have* to put up the tree, James."

"I know, but we can't dump all our traditions in the same year! I'll be back in an hour."

"Okay. Don't get lost, it's a jungle out there."

With the salad, steaks, and potatoes put away I made a cup of tea, grabbed my Bible and notebook, and settled in to my cozy black corner chair. I'd postponed my usual devotional time to get my shopping done. I pulled my green Afghan around my shoulders and opened the Christmas devotional book I'd worked on all month.

Today's passage was appropriately from Luke 2:4-6. I could almost recite it from memory: *Joseph also went up from Galilee, out of the city of Nazareth, into Judea, to the city of David, which is called Bethlehem, because he was of the house and lineage of David to be registered with Mary, his betrothed wife, who was with child. So it was, that while they were there, the days were completed for her to be delivered."* (NKJV)

I always identified with Mary in this passage, being hugely pregnant as I had been with David. And how comfortable could riding a donkey be even if you're not pregnant! How terrifying to have your baby delivered by strangers that happened by, or worse yet, a nervous Joseph!

Strangers! The word struck my mind like a lightning bolt! There was someone missing in this story. Someone who ordinarily would have been there. Someone who would want to be in Bethlehem with Mary on that night Jesus was born.

Where was Mary's mom?

For the first time I realized . . . Mary's mom was *at home* when her daughter gave birth to Jesus, her grandson.

I had read that in Biblical culture, mothers and aunts all helped the new mother. They got together to offer support during labor and delivery, cleaning the newborn, teaching breastfeeding and anything else a new mom might need. Mary's mom might have felt this kind of love and comfort when she gave birth to Mary and hoped to do the same for her own daughter one day

But Mary's mom was not in Bethlehem when Jesus was born. She could not imagine her daughter pregnant before marriage. Even if Mary's mom believed Mary was pure, no doubt she felt the stares of neighbors in the market and heard the gossip on the street. She most likely did not plan on preparing a hasty wedding, or setting her ripely-pregnant daughter on a donkey with her new son-in-law to take a seven-day trip to be registered. Mary's mom did not know exactly where or when her grandson was born. She could only imagine her daughter's cries of pain during labor — not knowing if anyone other than Joseph cared. She would not see the tiny bundle in Mary's arms or smell his sweet breath. No matter, she could welcome her grandchild when Mary and Joseph returned.

No one could have predicted Herod's bloodthirsty ego would force Mary and Joseph to take a three-year detour into Egypt before returning home. Did Mary's mom know where they were? Did she think they had been murdered by Herod's soldiers, or was Mary able to send a message that they were safe? How old was Jesus when his grandma first met him? Four? Five? When she saw him, did the ache of all the time she missed in his life start to fade?

I sat in my chair, humbled. I was complaining about my far-flung family but this grandma at the very first Christmas had to rely on God's promise and her prayers for comfort.

"I'm so sorry, Lord," I prayed, closing my hands over my Bible. "Mary's mom had so much more to deal with. I can call my kids. I can hear their voices. I know where they are. I know who they're with. Thank you that I don't have to wonder in darkness where my children might be. Thank you for the courage of this unknown woman who raised a daughter more righteous than most. Thank you for her brave trust that you would return her daughter to her."

My phone buzzed and a picture of my daughter's face with "Incoming Call" filled the screen. I marveled at how easy it is to hear her voice.

I answered the call. "Hi Lovey."

~ 24 ~

Silent Night with Blue Eyes

Stacey Longo Graham

When Sarah was told that in one year she would be with child, she laughed.

At ninety years of age, Sarah held her newborn baby.

If you had told me a year ago that while some people do last minute decorating, others sip hot chocolate, or still others chitchat before the Christmas Eve service starts, I would be thinking about rearranging the gnomes and elf that keep watch over the presents under the Christmas tree, I'd have laughed. Yet, instead, I remember Blue Eyes greeting me this morning and trying, as she ate breakfast, to hide the anxiety that the presents with her name on them will disappear before she gets to open them tomorrow.

Life is like that — full of plans, busyness, anxiety; yet we forget to just be.

Forget texting; remember to call. Trust me; sometimes a text won't do. I'll never forget the day the call came to us. "We're on our way" was all I could think to say. My husband never hesitated. She's family.

New house, new school, new friends, new family: She rarely complains, yet her whole world changed the day the ambulance came and took her mother away forever. Now, months later, this has also been the year for new Christmas routines.

Me, I think of all I could be doing. My husband and I were a childless couple with retirement looming on the horizon. Normally, instead of exchanging gifts, we would go camping or take a short trip returning on Christmas Eve, or travel right before New Year's. No, I'm not a scrooge wishing a child to be gone; I just wish two other eyes could be the ones looking at her. Instead, I try not to cry when she delights in Saturday morning pancakes, humbly fills an Operation Christmas Child shoebox, or hurriedly dresses for her first-ever Black Friday shopping day.

My tears fell earnestly, though, after she jumped from the truck and ran up the driveway with the news she's to be Dorothy Gayle, as in *Wizard of Oz*'s Dorothy, the ghost of Christmas future in the county theater's Christmas play. We danced with abandon right there in the driveway under the starry night sky. I know Jesus was right there with my husband, laughing and smiling. Even when I was exhausted after a long week, I was still right there at her play for all five performances. Relatives, friends, and teachers also came.

When I'm overwhelmed, frustrated, and think my patience is about gone, I close my eyes and visualize the licking lips as we watch the oven timer count down on the Christmas cookies, the speechless awe the first time my husband flipped the switch on the indoor Christmas lights, and her intense focus as she caressed the photo ornaments I handed her to add to the tree — ornaments with pictures of her and her mother. I think of the stockings hanging from the white wooden stocking box my brother made because a stocking is something she always had.

Stop. No. Right now, I keep my eyes wide open. I focus. I listen. It's the Christmas Eve service. I see Blue Eyes standing alone at the front of the sanctuary lit by candlelight as she sings the first verse of "Silent Night" before the crowd begins to join in, and my own blue eyes dim with mist. She was given the honor to close us out tonight, a babe in a manger and an orphan who led.

This has indeed been the year for new Christmas routines.

~ 25 ~

Location, Location, Location

Lori Williams

The story hit the news cycle at ten and five-year-old Ruthie called me at eleven. "Miss Lori, a fire burned the children's building," she said, her voice wobbly with worry. "Where will we have music class?"

"I know," I said as I pictured Ruthie with her big eyes peeking behind pale, wispy bangs. "But did you also hear that no one was hurt? And the firemen got to the church really fast?"

"But where will we have music class?" she persisted.

"We'll find a place," I said, my heart breaking and rejoicing at the same time. Oh, to have such a tender heart that craves worship! Oh, to be a child again . . .

"I promise, Ruthie," I said as much to her as to myself, "we'll find a place."

And find a place we did, in a cozy corner of the main church building. But I confess that Ruthie's question challenged me. Is our worship dependent on a place?

Does the One we worship ever relocate or get burned out?

The Christmas story answers that question for us.

Isaiah 7:14 (NIV) tells us, *The Lord himself will give you a sign: The virgin will conceive and give birth to a son, and will call him Immanuel.* Seven hundred years later that prophecy came true when Jesus was born in Bethlehem to a virgin named Mary (Matthew 1:23). Both of these passages mention the name Immanuel, which means "God with us."

Though just as glorious, the names "Wonderful Counselor, Mighty God, Everlasting Father and Prince of Peace" from Isaiah 9:6 are not repeated by Matthew. Could that be because only a God who is always with us could be those very things to us? The God who is always with us is the God we worship. Our worship of Him transcends our location.

I've felt God's presence with me more times and places than I can count. Ones that come to mind include gardens, at my oncologist's office, while feeding hummingbirds, at my piano, holding a friend who is brokenhearted, driving through Olympic National Park, singing and dancing with preschoolers like Ruthie, lighting candles on Christmas Eve, dipping my toes in the Indian Ocean, and especially, while attending my beloved husband's funeral. Worship of the one true God transcends grief, joy, wonder, awe, and even the indescribable. Because God came to us in the form of His Son Jesus, who then sent the Holy Spirit, we are never alone.

This Christmas the children and I will likely still be meeting in a small classroom without space for all our instruments and what I used to think were necessary trappings for worship. The fussy babies on the other side of the wall used to be down the hall and out of earshot. What seem like inconveniences are actually lessons for my grown-up heart. After all, the stable wasn't the ideal place for Jesus' birth, was it? Or, come to think of it, perhaps it was, because it was in that ordinary, extraordinary, setting that Jesus said, "I come to earth to be with you. There is no place too lowly, stinky, dark, out-of-the-way or unexpected where I am not present."

There is no location, location, location where He is not with us.

~ 26 ~

The Bracelet Promise

Carmen Leal

The glitter of green stones drew me to the solitary display case. The light bounced off the silver and glass. Amidst the jumble of holiday shoppers, I made my way to the corner area reserved for fine jewelry and gazed upon the bracelet, noticing the unique handiwork. The beaten silver, fashioned in such a way as to resemble diamond chips, was delightful. Seeing dozens of dark green emeralds, I knew this was a one-of-a-kind treasure.

As I stared in wonder at the intricate piece, I remembered a promise my husband had made. David had bought me a lovely gift four years before on our honeymoon. He had selected an emerald green Austrian crystal and seed pearl bracelet in honor of my May birthstone. As he fastened it on my wrist, he lovingly said, "I promise you that soon I will buy you real emeralds. Just wait." Though I loved the honeymoon gift, deep down I looked forward to David's promise.

Until that time however, I still delighted in wearing the delicate creation. I wore it frequently, each time remembering the island boutique. Whenever David saw the bracelet, he remembered his promise, and would reassure me that the time was coming soon when he would keep it.

It became our habit over the years to look in every jewelry store window as if searching for the Holy Grail. We wandered in and out of countless shops, becoming discouraged when we realized the cost of the promise was well beyond our means. I soon wavered in my belief that I would ever own what David desired to give me. However, David never lost faith.

Now we were in the mall during the last week before Christmas to buy gifts for our children. Finances were tight; we had agreed there would be no exchange of gifts between us. We had just completed one of the most stressful years possible. With David's diagnosis of Huntington's disease, our lives had forever changed. This terminal, neurological disorder had pitched us into a panic, not to mention near bankruptcy.

I looked up from the case into David's eyes and saw love shining even brighter than the stones. I could tell in his mind that nothing short of this bracelet would satisfy his honeymoon promise, but I knew there was no way we could possibly afford it. I tried to tell him but the words died on my lips. He he'd had so many disappointments this year, I didn't have the heart to tell him the answer was no.

Thinking fast, I came up with a reason to decline what I knew was an offer I could not accept. I have large wrists and normally bracelets don't fit. As the store clerk reverently lifted the object out of the case, I knew it would be too small.

The silver and green made a colorful contrast against my brown skin. I silently acknowledged how much I wanted this bracelet while hoping it would not fit. As the clerk reached around my wrist and closed the intricate clasp, my heart both plummeted and leapt. It fit! It was perfect, yet I knew there was no way we could afford it. The unpaid bills, with more looming in the future, had placed a vise around our checkbook.

I glanced at my best friend and saw his shining smile burst forth. This man, who had never hurt anyone, was now the victim of one of the cruelest diseases known to man. His was a sentence with only one verdict. Death. Untimely, slow, and cruel death. My eyes brimmed with tears as I realized we would not live out our dream of growing old together. To David, this was not just one more bauble in an already overcrowded jewelry box. Rather, this was his love displayed on my arm for all the world to see. To David, a promise made was a promise kept. I sadly realized that he might not have many more months or years to keep his promise. Suddenly it became the most important covenant ever made. Somehow, I had to juggle the bills to let him have the honor of keeping his promise.

"Do you like it?" he whispered. Hearing the hope in his voice, mingled with seeing the love in his eyes, was something I am sure few women ever have the privilege of experiencing. It was clear that David cherished me. All he ever wanted, from the day we met, was to please me.

"Yes, honey, I love it." I answered. "It's exactly what I want."

The clerk reached for my arm to remove the bracelet. I could not believe this little object had worked its way into my heart so quickly. "How much is it?" I finally asked. Slowly the man turned over the little white tag. Two-hundred-fifty dollars it read. Surely it was a mistake! I had seen enough to know that price was only a fraction of its worth.

The man began to extol the virtues of the item pointing out the one hundred and eighty emeralds in a hand-made Brazilian setting. But even though two-hundred-fifty dollars was an incredible price, it might as well have been $2,500.00, for all we could stretch our meager budget. Without thinking I asked, "Would you take two hundred twenty-five dollars, tax included?" Shops in malls do not normally bargain, but the words tumbled out of my mouth. He looked at me in surprise and answered, "That will be fine."

Before he could change his mind, I whipped out my credit card, all the while watching as David beamed with pride. The man quickly handled the transaction and we were on our way. Every few steps we would stop and look at the bracelet. Before we reached the car, David said, "When I get sicker and eventually die, you need to look at each emerald. Each one will remind you of something special we've done. A trip we took, a movie we saw, or a moment we shared. This will be your memory bracelet." I began to cry. David's concern was not his own failing health but for how I would handle life without him.

As we worked our way home in the bumper-to-bumper traffic of rush-hour Honolulu, I wondered just how we could pay for the bracelet. Oddly enough I never really panicked, I was just somehow curious how it would all work out. We talked as we travelled and every so often looked at the miracle of the promise kept.

On the way into the house I grabbed the mail and began to open it as we walked inside. Amidst the usual bills were two cards. I opened the first which was from a church where I had sung several times that year. It was a thank you note for my music ministry . . . along with a gift. I was speechless. I was looking at a check for two hundred dollars! I reached for the second card and slit it open. Out fell two bills; a twenty and a five. The card was simply signed, "A friend in Christ."

I looked up at David and we both began to laugh. I remembered how I had felt the need to ask the clerk if he would take two-hundred twenty-five dollars, tax included. Even as we were in the mall, the payment for David's promise was in the mailbox. God had already taken care of every detail, including the twenty-five dollars plus tax.

It is just a piece of jewelry. Something I could have lived without. But the memories attached to our time together have helped to make me the woman I am today. The exquisite joy and the unspeakable grief of this relationship have grown me in ways I could never have anticipated. The promise David spoke on our honeymoon had been fulfilled. It was only through God that we stopped at that shop on that day to find that specific bracelet. The pastor of a small church, coupled with an unknown friend, listened to God as they decided their holiday giving.

Before I was ever born, God made another promise. He promised me eternal salvation. He promised He would be with me every step of the way. All I had to do was ask. Just as God never stopped believing I would claim that first promise, David never stopped believing in his bracelet promise. When I wear my emeralds, I pull out memories I have tucked away in my heart. I also remember David's faith and God's promises.

~ 27 ~

Marry Christmas from Moldova

Terri Elders

When Elvira, the Peace Corps Moldovan health project manager, suggested that Angela would be a suitable pen pal for my stepson, Rick, I hesitated. I was in Chisinau to review the health project. After visiting schools and orphanages, we'd taken a supper break. Over a succulent pork stew and *mamaliga*, the traditional cornbread, we chatted about Internet romances. Elvira told me how a friend met a Frenchman online and eventually married him. I countered with how a Russian hairdresser had pressured Rick to send money for exorbitant alleged internet café charges.

"Rick should write to Angela," Elvira said, after I'd met the executive assistant to the Peace Corps director. Angela had impressed me with her thoughtfulness and energy.

"Hmmm, I don't know," I replied. As much as I treasure *Hello, Dolly* and *Fiddler on the Roof*, I believe marriages are made in heaven, that mere earthlings lack needed acumen to match strangers.

I recalled once hosting a Christmas party where a couple of my guests met and started to date. They'd lavished me with thanks. When it became apparent that one was a spendthrift and the other a penny pincher, the relationship turned sour. Both parties blamed me, even though my matchmaking had been inadvertent.

I agreed to speak to Rick, though, and described Angela to him. She held a master's degree and had worked variously as a librarian, teacher, and administrator. She claimed Moldovan men either lacked ambition or were overly fond of the local cognac and wine. Tall and pretty, she had thick curly light brown hair and a ready smile.

"I wouldn't mind writing," Rick said. "She sounds great. I'll have to explain, though, how busy I am and that my letters might be infrequent and brief."

Besides his full-time meat department work at Costco, and occasional substitute teaching, Rick was completing his MA in Education. He'd tried dating but found the local pickings slim. While he was nearing forty, most available women were in their twenties and into discos and pub crawls. Those closer in age sought ready-made fathers to support their already-established families.

Rick envisioned a wife and kids in his future, he confided, but he wanted to finish his education first. "I still have time before the parade passes by. But I pray I'll find somebody who shares my beliefs, interests, and my faith."

Over the next two years Rick and Angela exchanged e-mails. She wrote of trips to London and Edinburgh for her new job with the British Embassy, and of how frigid her apartment grew at night in early spring after the government turned off the heat. He wrote of term papers and exams, his Bible study group, and his progress landscaping his Nevada home.

"There's never a trace of romance in those exchanges," Ken, my husband, commented after Rick forwarded some of the e-mails. I shrugged. "Matchmaking's not my strong point," I reminded him.

In the meantime, I retired, and my husband and I moved to rural Northeast Washington, where Rick, too, eventually wanted to relocate. One autumn day I came in from picking apples and sat down at the computer. I opened a message from Rick and read that Angela had invited him to visit her at Christmas. Instead, he had offered to pay for her to come to the States for the holidays if she could get a visa. "I've explained that we'll celebrate Christmas with you and Dad in the country, so make sure you provide snow."

We welcomed company for our first Christmas in our new home. When we attended local holiday crafts fairs, we always picked up a scarf or a pair of mittens for Angela. "Poor thing," Ken would say, "She has to boil water for her daily bath." He admired her already, sight unseen, for her endurance in dealing with the hardships of living in a developing country.

In early December I received an electronic greeting card from ever-optimistic Elvira. "Wishing you a Marry Christmas," she wrote. I laughed aloud. "I wouldn't bet on it," I wrote back. "I think this is just a case of two lonely people being kind to one another."

When Rick and Angela arrived early on Christmas Eve, to my relief, it had already begun to snow. Though we'd had a dusting at Thanksgiving, there'd been none since. I despaired that I'd be unable to supply the white Christmas Rick had requested.

While Angela took her bags to her guest room, Rick confided that she'd walked right up to him at the airport. She'd hit it off with all his friends and neighbors, he said when she'd cooked everybody a tasty chicken dinner. "Some suggested I should marry her," he added, grinning. Ken cocked his eyebrow and glanced my way.

By afternoon, we'd had heavy snowfall. Nonetheless, Rick and Angela took a walk around the neighborhood anyway. The loop we lived on had many homes decorated for the season.

While I set the table, Ken mentioned that they both seemed smitten. "He was holding her hand," he said.

I hadn't noticed. "They're just friends," I answered.

Christmas morning, we opened our presents. Angela loved her scarlet mittens and the chocolates in the mini-stockings I had hung on the door to her room. She gave us the same cognac that graced the tables of lavish Moscow diplomatic dinners in the days of the former USSR.

We taught her to play hearts, and she tried to teach us to play durac, a Russian card game. "Durac" means stupid, Angela explained, but we were too stupid to master it.

We told Angela about Rudolph and Santa Claus, and she shared stories of Kindly Grandfather Krechun, an Eastern European character who delivers fir trees and gifts. Myth claims that baby Jesus was born at his house, she explained.

Rick cornered me in the kitchen as I began to peel potatoes. "I'm going to ask her to marry me," he said. I dropped the peeler. "She's perfect," he added. "Just perfect. She might feel the same way about me."

They took another walk. It took only twenty minutes to circle the loop, so after an hour I peered out the front window at the snowy landscape. I saw Rick and Angela approach our house then wheel to go back the other way.

When they returned, Rick announced we needed to break out the wine to toast the spouses-to-be. "I asked her how she would feel about living in the States," he said, "And she asked how I would feel about having a wife."

Angela prepared *mamaliga* to accompany our holiday feast.

They married that May in Serpenti, her Moldovan village.

We shared many Christmases, always playing hearts, never durac. Angela never mentioned our inability to learn. The snow always began to fall on Christmas Eve. Rick and Angela always walked around the loop, holding hands.

Ken passed away sixteen years ago, so eventually, I returned to my native California. Rick and Angela moved to Arizona, where he's a teacher and she's a nurse.

This past summer, their daughter, Kendra, born just three weeks after Ken's death, turned sixteen. Days later, I joined them at their vacation condo in Oceanside where we played hearts. Kendra has picked up her grandfather's skill.

I've yet to learn to play durac. Who knows? I'm not too old or stupid to learn.

I have proof now that marriages *are* made in heaven. Angela was heaven-sent, the answer to Rick's prayers. Me? I got the granddaughter I'd always dreamed of.

~ 28 ~

Wrappings

Joanna K. Harris

I search for the perfect gift,
The one just right, that says,
    You're remembered.
    You're valued.
    You're loved.
Then I wrap it up in red and gold,
With silky ribbon and a sparkly bow,
Anticipating my loved one's response —
The smile, the delight, the happy hug!
Such joy in giving a gift
Which says more than words can say.

Traditions come and customs go,
But I give because I first received.

Almighty God gave the first gift, the best,
His only Son, come down to earth —
    Wrapped in humanity.
    Wrapped in humility.
    Wrapped in ordinary.

Exhausted mother, ecstatic father,
Tiny baby laid in a manger.
Sparkling star, shepherds kneeling,
Wise men with gold bringing.
A Savior born — God with us,
The perfect gift to say,
    You are remembered.
    You are valued.
    You are loved.

Now wrapped in grace, in peace,
In blessings eternal, I give myself to Him.

~ 29 ~

Swaddling Clothes

Suzanne D. Nichols

I watched my daughter lay her newborn daughter across a folded, cotton blanket. In three or four well-executed movements, she snugged the baby's arms close to her body and secured her into what resembled a blanket cocoon, leaving only the child's head visible.

Baby swaddling has regained popularity during the past several years. Pediatricians, hospital nurseries, and new mothers have rediscovered the soothing effects nighttime swaddling brings to newborns, and even to babies several months old.

As my daughter gently laid her sleeping infant into the bassinette, I envisioned another mother kneeling beside a manger to place the newborn baby Jesus onto a cushion of cattle feed (Luke 2:7). In a shelter meant for animals, God provided safety, privacy, and comfort for this child — His Son — and Mary trusted His every move.

When an angel of the Lord appeared to shepherds watching over their sheep in the fields outside Bethlehem, the messenger gave only brief clues for finding the newborn Savior — *This shall be a sign unto you: Ye shall find the babe wrapped in swaddling clothes, lying in a manger* (Luke 2:12 KJV).

The shepherds immediately went in search of the child. But a deeper examination of Hebrew tradition reveals they may have known exactly where to look.

If these shepherds were of the special group trained to care for the lambs meant for Passover and for Temple sacrifices, they realized the significance of the angel's clues.

When ewes were ready to give birth, they were moved to special birthing caves kept ritually pure for that purpose. Lambs born for sacrifice were to be without blemish. Many scholars believe the shepherds swaddled the wobbly newborns to protect them against injury and ensure their perfection.

The angel's clues also matched the proclamation, *Today in the town of David, a Savior has been born to you; He is Christ the Lord* (Luke 2:11 KJV). The shepherds recognized the fulfillment of prophecy because they understood the symbolism in the circumstances. And so, directed by the angel's brief instructions, they set out in search of what they envisioned: the promised Messiah, newly-born and swaddled as a perfect lamb, cradled in a feed trough in a ceremonially pure cave, in the prophesied city of Bethlehem.

And that is indeed what they found.

* * * * *

My newborn granddaughter awoke in the early-morning hours, vocalizing her demands. I peeked into the room to see if the new mom needed my help only to find her laughing at her baby girl whose arms now rested above her downy head, free from the retrains of the swaddle.

I thought again of Mary as she gazed at the perfection of her newborn. I wondered if she imagined what His arms would hold in the future. Those arms — somewhat restricted by swaddling clothes in those moments — would later reach out to heal, comfort, and redeem the world.

From Genesis to Revelation, we can trace the crimson thread of God's salvation plan as He reveals His marvelous gift to those who seek after truth. As did the shepherds, I respond to the angel's good news of great joy and I come to worship Him — Christ the Lord, Lamb of God, heaven's perfect sacrifice.

~ 30 ~

It Started with Bananas

Cecil Taylor

Paw Paw was irritated. Despite his protests, he got stuck babysitting four of his grandchildren while their grandmother and mother went shopping on Christmas Eve. And in a mixture of dead seriousness and serious silliness, Paw Paw encountered a moment in which the two intersected.

I was the oldest of those grandchildren. I noticed Paw Paw rooting around in the kitchen. He returned with a bunch of bananas, fished out string from his large oak desk with its many drawers, and set out tying individual bananas on the Christmas tree as ornaments. He alternated between grumbling and chuckling evilly.

When the shoppers got home, of course, we children tattled on our grandpa. "Look what Paw Paw did! He tied bananas on the Christmas tree!"

Grandma and Mama stared at the yellow adornments, hardly believing that a man finicky about tree decoration would do such a thing. "Why did you do that?" they asked.

"Because you left me home alone with these children!" he exclaimed. "That's what happens when you leave like that!"

The bananas remained on the tree. I could hardly wait for

Uncle John to arrive the next day for our family celebration. Uncle John was like his father, so fastidious about the appearance of his Christmas tree; he had the habit of delicately laying hundreds of icicles individually across the branches. How would Uncle John react to bananas?

The moment was as delicious as a perfectly ripe banana. Uncle John greeted the family, seated himself on the sofa, and gazed approvingly at the tree's shape. "That's a mighty fine tree you have, Daddy," he said. Then his demeanor changed: a confused look, squinty eyes, a couple of blinks, a twist of the head, his neck bobbing his head to look top to bottom, a frown assembling with its center between his eyebrows.

"Daddy, are those bananas on the tree?" he cautiously inquired.

"Yep," said Paw Paw, "and they're on there because I had to babysit the grandkids yesterday!"

Uncle John chose to ask no further questions.

We have a family phrase: If you do it twice, it's a tradition.

A tradition was formed the next year when we grandchildren insisted on draping something silly on the Christmas tree. We managed to hang nuts in tiny mesh bags to clearly represent that our family was nuts. The next year, the decorations were golf balls and tees. Clothespins and tea packets made appearances in subsequent holiday seasons.

For a while, the tradition served as a way to needle someone who had fouled up during the year. Sometimes that was well accepted, but sometimes not. One year, I had an issue while baking pumpkin pie; I didn't properly separate eggs, so egg separators were attached to the tree in my honor. In recent years, I ordered a case of ice cream cups to ship to my father. But I entered the address carelessly and shipped them to myself. I accepted the inevitable punishment and saved all the cup lids as I ate my way through the case, then I hung them from the tree myself.

Nature took its turn inspiring the tree tradition over the years. Way-too-close family member incidents with squirrels and birds were commemorated with special ornaments.

Sweet moments also made their way onto the tree. After my son and daughter-in-law got engaged one October, the Christmas tree greeted them with shiny rings spinning underneath its branches. When my wife mustered the courage to finally try ziplining, we strung beads around the tree with miniature snowmen ziplining their way down.

The classic misadventure leading to a tree memory did not involve a single individual, but two families. That summer, we visited our six-year-old daughter's godparents in west Texas. She developed a rash, so her mother and godmother took her to the emergency room. The quick diagnosis, without much inspection, was scabies, an infestation of a microscopic skin mite.

Under doctor's orders, we fumigated the house, setting off a bug bomb and leaving for hours. That evening, we coated ourselves from hair tips to toenails with a creamy medicine, stuck that night to the bedsheets, and lined up for showers and bedsheet laundering the next morning. The scabies outbreak seemed to be defeated.

Waving goodbye to the godparents after the hassle of scabies treatment, our family headed across state to the beach. I noticed my daughter's rash was back. Once again visiting the nearest ER, a doctor gave a correct diagnosis this time: She was allergic to an ingredient in our suntan lotion! What a laugh we had with her very understanding godparents when we revealed the scabie drill was for naught.

That December, we bought little alien-looking rubber bugs and wedged them into the Christmas tree to commemorate a difficult, sticky, unnecessary episode in west Texas.

You may think we're bananas for hanging unusual items on the tree. I can't argue. I'm thinking it's about time to decorate with actual bananas again this Christmas as a remembrance of how our odd tradition started.

~ 31 ~

Christmas on a Mountain Farm

Victoria Barker

My childhood Christmases were spent at my grandparents' farm, in the mountains of Eastern Kentucky. My mother was one of eleven children, so the small house was often overflowing with people. Since I was an only child, it was a happy change from my life in the city. When we arrived, often late at night, we parked at a small store across from a path that led down a steep, rocky slope toward a roaring creek. My father carried a flashlight as we crossed the creek on a swinging bridge.

I was terrified of this bridge, so I rarely looked down at the water below. My parents and I next crossed a large corn field and then began climbing our way up a hill toward the house. It was surrounded by a fence, which also enclosed a smokehouse, cellar, and well. As we approached the back door, the smells began to wash over me.

The first scent came from the cast iron cook stove just inside the kitchen door. It was wood-fired, and whatever it yielded had a smoky taste. The fragrance was wonderful and part of a layered aroma which included the three coal burning fireplaces on the first floor of the home. The odor of burning coal was earthy, acrid, and musky; it clung to everything inside.

If it was early in the evening, we were welcomed with lots of hugs and shouts of, "Merry Christmas!" If everyone was asleep, we tiptoed upstairs to our bedroom, where all three of us slept together on a feather mattress. During the day, when it was not mealtime, the family gathered in my grandparents' bedroom. It was our den, and it was filled with rocking chairs and a fireplace with a big mantle. There were also a television and radio, but we rarely listened unless it was time for the programs with Gospel hymns that Grandmother loved. Next to this bedroom was the "parlor" and dining room where there were boxes of fudge and bowls of oranges and tangerines. I thought the taste of peanut butter fudge and tangerines was heavenly. After my grandparents went to bed, I liked to settle in where the talk was most interesting; this was often in the parlor, where my aunts and uncles shared stories.

When I was young, there was never a Christmas tree until after I arrived and begged for one. Then my uncle would go to the woods and come back with a cedar tree, just the right size. If no one else was interested in decorating the tree, the joy was mine. I hung the antique, glass ornaments as high as my arms could reach. My mother would help when it was time to hang the Star of Bethlehem.

On Christmas morning, it was usually very cold; the window panes and doorknobs would be crusted with frost until the fires were blazing again. After a prayer of thanks for our food, we often had a breakfast of country ham, biscuits, plum jam, eggs, and fried apples, everything home-grown. After breakfast, I loved to bundle up and wander around the farm. My cousins and I liked to follow a path past the chicken house and around the edge of the property to where the "old house" once stood. There was still a barn close by, but we were cautioned not to go inside because it contained a jumble of farm equipment and was not a good place to play.

After wandering, we'd go home to a wonderful lunch of foods brought in by the family. We ate turkey roasted in the cast iron stove. We also had cornbread dressing, green beans with ham, baked potatoes, and buttered corn, and fried apples. We didn't watch television or play games. I sometimes played with a big box of sea shells that an uncle had brought home from a far-away beach, but most of the time, we simply talked. I liked the stories about my family and times past; I wanted to know about those great-grandparents whose pictures hung on the walls. I listened and learned. I discovered the strength of my grandmother's faith when she asked us to read the Bible. She especially liked the account of the conversion of Paul and would later ask me questions about this story to make sure I understood. These were my favorite times because I felt surrounded by the faith and strength of my family.

It was rare for Christmas gifts to be exchanged. My grandparents were older and not inclined to shop for so many people. Only once, after most guests had left, they gave me a small wooden chest filled with chocolates. I was thrilled to receive this, but my favorite gifts were hearing the stories and laughter of my family. As I grew older, I was grateful for the heritage of faith that sustained my grandparents, and to learn about their salvation experiences and how they prayed for me. The abiding love that surrounded our gatherings was real, and I now realize how rare it is to have a family that loved each other so well. My grandparents' faith was the reason, and Jesus was their Sustainer, Hope, and their source of Peace.

~ 32 ~

My Favorite Christmas Tradition

Ben Cooper

As the ever-spinning clock and calendar race their way to December 25th, songs, scenery, and spirits transform into a more positive atmosphere. Store shopping sprees, holiday concerts, and family gatherings all compete for our time. Baking, tree trimming, and Christmas parties abound. Movies, music, and mindsets gear up to familiar tempos. Our cultural and familial traditions materialize with thoughts focused on the people we treasure. Christian believers join in with their "must have" moments.

My family's traditions include a Christmas Eve candlelight service, followed by opening our stockings, and topped off with watching *It's a Wonderful Life*. Christmas morning begins with breaking the early morning silence with the volume cranked up on Manheim Steamrollers version of "Joy to the World." The television screen becomes a Yuletide fireplace, and we find our places among the brightly packaged gifts.

But before anyone opens a present, a tradition my wife started thirty years ago when our children were young helps us realize the best gift ever given. Three large envelopes holding cardstock with words and a few graphic images are passed out to willing readers.

Christmas Letter One

For unto us [Dad, Mom, Wesley, Haydn, Sean, Grace, and Suzanna] *a Child is born. Unto us a Son is given"* (Isaiah 9:6 NKJV).

She will bring forth a Son and you shall call His name Jesus, for He will save His people [Dad, Mom, Wesley, Haydn, Sean, Grace, and Suzanna] *from their sins* (Matthew 1:21 NKJV).

For God so loved the world that He gave His only begotten Son, that whoever [Dad, Mom, Wesley, Haydn, Sean, Grace, and Suzanna] *believes in Him should not perish but have everlasting life* (John 3:16 NKJV).

Christmas Letter Two

Christ also suffered once for all sins, the just and the unjust, that He might bring us [Dad, Mom, Wesley, Haydn, Sean, Grace, and Suzanna] *to God, being put to death in the flesh but made alive by the Spirit* (1 Peter 3:18 NKJV).

Who Himself bore our [Dad, Mom, Wesley, Haydn, Sean, Grace, and Suzanna] *sins in His own body on the tree, that we, having died to sins might live for righteousness – by Whose stripes you were healed* (1 Peter 2:24 NKJV).

Christmas Letter Three

Jesus said to her, "I am the resurrection and the life. He [Dad, Mom, Wesley, Haydn, Sean, Grace, and Suzanna] *who believes in Me, though he may die, he shall live"* (John 11:25 NKJV).

If you confess with your mouth the Lord Jesus and believe in your heart that God has raised Him from the dead, you [Dad, Mom, Wesley, Haydn, Sean, Grace, and Suzanna] *will be saved* (Romans 10:9 NKJV).

As changes in our family numbers and dynamics come, additional names appear. When the kids were younger, they waited as Mom and Dad read each Christmas letter. Our children are all adults now and live on their own. Yet they still look forward to the Christmas letters and happily volunteer to read one of them. When spouses and grandchildren eventually come along, their names will be added to the personalized portion of the Christmas letters.

I expect that one day, my wife will create copies for each of our kids to have Christmas letters read in their own homes, expanding the precious tradition she started years ago for future generations.

What is your unique Christmas family tradition? Are you sharing it with your family and friends? If you don't have a special tradition, consider incorporating one that presents the best gift of all, Emanuel, God with us.

It seems fitting to end with a quote from my wife's favorite Charlie Brown character, Linus: "That's what Christmas is all about!"

Keep Christ the central part of your Christmas traditions.

~ 33 ~
Remember the Child

Leigh Ann Thomas

What is that sound?
Is it the sound of Christmas?

The steady shuffle of weary feet,
The grumbling of overworked, overtired parents,
Cries from children demanding the trinket of the moment.

What *is* that sound?
Shoppers scrambling for the elusive, hoped-for gift,
The captivating call of media
Promising gold-hued, paper-thin fulfillment.
The sights and sounds of Christmas . . .

If we look and listen a little more,
We see cherub faces, pink from a recent scrubbing,
Representing characters in a story from long ago.
We see a choir — rehearsed and dressed in matching apparel,
Singing about a child of lowly birth.

We see a room, alight with the glow of candles,
Inhale the scent of freshly baked goodies,
Delight in the laughter and love of family and friends.

*But if our hunger for Christmas is real,
And our thirst for Truth runs deep,
Perhaps we should look even closer
And listen even harder . . .*

Envision a night of exquisite beauty,
With the only source of light, a star-filled sky.
Listen — and hear the shallow breathing of shepherds
And the gentle bleating of sheep.

Feel the emotions of a new father and mother
As their eyes meet and they silently rejoice in awe and wonder.
Behold the look of radiance on a virgin mother's face
As she holds an infant, soft in sleep.

Reach and touch newborn skin,
Feel the baby's warm breath on your hand.
And as you touch,
Know that you are touching
The Son of God.

Be careful, lest the vision slip away . . .
Open your heart and let this most holy of nights
Enter your soul and change you forever.
And when the world threatens to overwhelm you,
And you feel like you're *drowning* in the season . . .

Remember the night,
Remember the sounds,
Remember the love,

Remember . . . *the Child.*

For God loved the world in this way: He gave His One and Only Son, so that everyone who believes in Him will not perish but have eternal life.
John 3:16 HCSB

~ 34 ~
Alone for Christmas?

Barbara D'Antoni Diggs

My family always celebrated Christmas with lots of people. One year, however, I lived ten hours away from them and couldn't afford to travel. Being the people-person that I was, the likelihood of being totally alone on Christmas Day left me a bit anxious and sad.

After work a few days before the holiday, I saw a freshly-cut Christmas tree on the porch of my tiny rental house. I wondered who put it there. I looked for a note, but didn't find one. I was excited to have my first, very own tree. Lugging it inside, I set about putting it up. I didn't have a stand; instead I nestled the tree in a large bucket, stuffed newspaper around the base and added water. It was lopsided and quite wobbly. I tied a rope around the middle of the tree, tossed it over the curtain rod and pulled it tight. As long as I didn't jiggle the tree too hard, I thought this would work.

Poorer than a church mouse, I didn't have decorations or lights for a tree. After work the next afternoon, I stopped by a thrift store and purchased a few ornaments. In addition, I made paper chains like when I was a kid. I also cut out magazine pictures and glued them onto construction paper to hang on the limbs. I nodded to myself, *This will give my tree some character.*

Putting on a Christmas album, I joyfully sang along as I decorated my tree. It didn't take me long. After two songs I was finished. My one string of lights didn't go far, but it did give a hint of twinkle throughout the tree.

I decided to place a family photo in the branches, too, since we wouldn't be together this year! The tree looked beautiful to me.

The following day, a large box arrived from my parents. In bold, black letters, the phrase "Do not open until December 25th" was written several times on the outside of the box. Even five hundred miles away, my parents were aware of my tendency to peek into gifts, and I knew they would ask me about it later.

As I planned my Christmas day, I decided it would be about celebrating Jesus' birthday and not a day of self-pity because I was alone. I started my celebration on Christmas Eve after the 6 P.M. church service by making a cup of hot chocolate, playing carols on the stereo, and sitting by my beautiful, lopsided tree. It was different and peaceful — but still, I felt a tinge of loneliness. Before going to bed that night, I set my alarm for 6 A.M.

The next morning, the first thing I did when I awoke was sing "Happy Birthday" to Jesus. Then, I read the Christmas story aloud. I thought through different Bible verses, sang hymns, and worshipped. It was delightful. I felt the presence of the Lord with me throughout the celebration. It surprised me how meaningful this time was. I didn't feel alone at all.

Because it was cold outside *and* inside of my poorly-insulated house, I splurged that morning and turned my wall heater up a little higher. I rarely used much heat because I couldn't afford it. But today was a celebration — thus, a tad more heat. Next, I made a cup of coffee and cozied up by my tree and the heater.

Suddenly, there was a loud banging on my door. When I opened it, there stood my best friend, Elaine. She had a big, beautifully-wrapped box and a covered picnic basket in her hand. "I brought eggs and cheese for omelets, bread for toast, and fresh strawberries to make us breakfast," she said. "But before that, you have to open my present."

She took the basket into the kitchen, then sat by me on the sofa. Excitedly, she handed me scissors, "Hurry, open it!" she said.

Oh my goodness! It's a stoneware dinner set for four! Elaine had a set in brown and I thought they were the neatest-looking dishes. Instead of my unmatched pieces from thrift stores, now I had a real set of dishes, too. She told me we had to wash them and use them for our breakfast.

Elaine headed to the kitchen to start preparing our food. In the meantime, I put red placemats and cloth napkins on the coffee table and even lit a few candles. I went to the kitchen to help, and soon we carried our meals out on my brand new plates. We got comfy on the living room floor beside the wall heater and barely-twinkling tree. Both of us thoroughly enjoyed our feast.

After breakfast, I remembered the box my parents had sent me. "Can you stay while I open it, or do you need to get to your family's house?" I asked. Elaine said she had time to stay.

Because I was barely scraping by financially, my parents had wrapped and sent all kinds of food and household supplies, including cans of tuna and soup, toilet paper, hot chocolate and margarine. Yes, my mother actually mailed me two tubs of margarine! And, yes, they melted. Fortunately, she'd wrapped them in plastic wrap, so the mess didn't get all over everything. My mother and I laughed about that gift for years.

Two other wonderful surprises were included in my box: a yellow 8-track tape player and a red cassette recorder. By using the recorder, we could send "talking" tapes back-and-forth, saving the expense of long-distance calls.

My first real Christmas alone was not at all like I thought it would be. Jesus and I celebrated Him and then, I feel like we had a party. I had my decorated mystery tree, Elaine came with breakfast, and I had boxes of gifts and food for the future. In addition, there also was the bonus of extra heat.

What a joyful Christmas day it turned out to be! I tried to make the day about Jesus instead of me. However, He showered me with so many surprise blessings to reflect on, I didn't remember I expected to be totally alone.

~ 35 ~
How to Cope Through the Season Alone

Donna Wyland

Christmas fantasies fill our minds with ornament-covered trees, laughter, and festive family dinners. But how do we survive — or even enjoy — the holiday season if our circumstances render us alone?

It was Christmas morning. The sun was shining, and the temperature was a mild forty degrees. After living with an emotionally abusive spouse for nearly fourteen years, I had moved to an undisclosed location to gain strength to face his addiction and improve my deteriorating health. I was thrilled with the relief this living arrangement had provided, but sometimes I felt very alone. Would I ever truly be loved? Would I be able to trust enough to love in return?

I'm happy to say that God answered that question with a resounding, "Yes!" I'm so excited about His encouragement to me. I pray that the God of all hope encourages you with His love, too, and that your Christmas season alone won't feel so lonely after all.

Here are tips I discovered that can fill your heart with holiday peace and joy:

- Be prepared. Most people know in advance if they will be spending the holidays alone. Forego the traditional Christmas Day meal if you prefer something else. Stock up on your favorite foods to enjoy . . . like pizza. Stock your favorite soda, coffee, or teas. Buy or borrow a great book or movie. Holiday comedies like *Last Holiday, Elf, Jingle All the Way, Christmas with the Kranks, Deck the Halls, It Happened on Fifth Avenue,* and *Christmas in Connecticut* truly are good for the body *and* soul.

- Spend time with God. If time with God is already a regular part of your schedule, wake up excited to read your Bible trusting that God has a special word of encouragement for you. Open the Word and trust Him to lead you to what He knows you need to hear for your heart to be filled with peace and hope for the New Year.

- Journal. Write your thoughts and feelings to express your experience, but before you begin to write, speak a word of gratitude to God. Direct your journal entries personally to God and end each one like a tender love letter. Tangible evidence of a thankful heart blesses not only the author but also God Himself. He delights in a grateful heart.

- Decorate if you're so inclined, but if you don't have the energy, don't. Maybe you don't want a Christmas tree this year. Instead, if you have some Christmas lights lying around, string a strand or two in the room where you spend the most time. Then set a nativity scene nearby, or hang a stocking where you can stack a few small wrapped gifts below, and enjoy the display. When the sun sets and all seems dark, the glow from those tiny lights will illuminate not only your home, but your heart and mind as well.

- Stay connected. If you receive phone calls, texts, emails, or any other form of communication, don't ignore them. Acknowledge concerned family and friends' messages and assure them you are alright. If you'd like to join friends or family for some holiday fun, by all means do so. Your heart will guide you to the decision that is best for you.

- Choose your Attitude. If you find your mind wandering to negative thoughts, be proactive. Switch your focus to a special memory, a humorous thought, or a person you enjoy. Grab a fun magazine or book to fill your mind with positive stimuli. An hour later you'll likely find that your attitude has dramatically improved.

- Take time to dream. New Year's Day is exactly one week after Christmas Day. A new year is about to begin. It's time to dream, set goals, and start a new chapter of your life. Set goals, large and small. Be specific. Decide to start a new hobby or join a class. *Jesus, Inc.*, by Laurie Beth Jones, is filled with encouragement and inspiration for anyone who is about to embark on a new adventure or take a new direction in life.

- Don't be afraid to try something new. I happened to attend an event where some women were talking about joining a line-dancing class. I love to dance, so I joined. I can't wait to pull on my old leather boots!

You *can* do all things through Christ who gives you strength! (Philippians 4:13) This Christmas you may feel lonely, but rest assured you are never truly alone. God goes before you, walks beside you, and covers every thought, action and word with His love.

Take steps to live intentionally, one day at a time.

Then, expect small miracles.

~ 36 ~

A Very Different Christmas

April G. Pope

While quarantining during Covid at Christmas, I decided to have a photoshoot with my animals on the farm. It did not go well.

Instead of standing in front of my wreath, Lottie (my now grown bottle lamb), ate the pinecones and pulled the wreath off of the barn. Gabe, my Great Pyrenees rolled over and played dead wearing his "PEACE" sign, and BB my ram, refused to look up towards the camera with his antlers on.

I suspect that just as my Christmas photoshoot was far from what I had imagined, many of our Christmas celebrations that year (and every year) are not going to resemble what the Hallmark movies tell us Christmas should be.

As tempting as it is to be upset or bitter, let's remind ourselves that if we are quarantined, if we are celebrating the first Christmas without a loved one, or if we just burn the turkey, the real meaning of Christmas does not change. In fact, maybe *because* of our circumstances we will focus on the spectacular simplicity of the very first Christmas. Mary would not have chosen to give birth to Jesus in a barn, but how magnificent that God chose to send our Savior to us in a way that showed the world that the Perfect Lamb was born in an imperfect place to fulfill God's perfect plan in a fallen world.

So do not despair! Our Eternal Hope, the greatest gift the world has ever known, was given to us under difficult, and very different circumstances.

She will bring forth a Son, and you shall call His name Jesus, for He will save His people from their sins. So all this was done that it might be fulfilled which was spoken by the Lord through the prophet, saying: "Behold, the virgin shall be with child, and bear a Son, and they shall call His name Immanuel," which is translated, "God with us."

Matthew 1:21-23 NKJV

~ 37 ~
A Priceless Gift for a Single Mom

Christina Ryan Claypool

Raising a child alone, I discovered what should have been the most festive season was often the greatest reminder of the absence of family in the traditional sense. Our modest Yuletide celebration didn't bear any resemblance to the sentimental TV commercials where loved ones gather around a large dining table laden with delicious steaming dishes and decorated with a poinsettia centerpiece and flickering candles. A scene where holiday music plays softly in the background. Ours probably looked more like Bob Cratchit's meager, although joyful celebration depicted in Charles Dickens' classic, *A Christmas Carol*.

Looking Back on Christmases Past

On Christmas Eve, it was usually just Zach and me, because my mother, stepfather, and most of our other relatives lived out of state. Despite this fact, when Zachary was young, I tried desperately to achieve some sense of Christmas cheer, while operating within a confining budget. I never expected any presents. Like many solo parents, I only cared that there would be something special under the tree for my precious youngster. Even the Christmas tree in our apartment was a hand-me-down from another once-single mom who had remarried and graduated to improved economic security.

Still, at Christmastime, I tried my best to make sure there were lots of packages for Zach to open. Not expensive items, just tiny tokens of how grateful I was to have been granted the privilege of raising him. My sensitive, dark-haired boy never expected much or complained there should have been more. He understood our situation.

Well, except for the year when he was three or four, and desperately wanted a specific toy I couldn't buy for him. It wasn't an extremely expensive item. Rather, it was a widely popular plastic car that was out of stock everywhere. It certainly wasn't a very merry Christmas tainted by my then toddler's tantrum and tears. It might have been the Christmas Zach first decided it was best not to desire material goods, since it was distressing and disappointing when those expectations were left unmet.

Every single parent's story is probably complicated, because real life can be messy. In my case, Zachary's father and I were married only briefly and for all the wrong reasons. Following our divorce mere months after our infant son was born, his dad moved back in with his parents. Yet Zach's late father always made sure his little boy had an impressive gift. Although the present usually remained at his dad's house awaiting their weekend visits. I wanted Zach to have toys and dreamed-of items at our apartment where he could enjoy them daily.

It Is More Blessed to Give than to Receive

Part of an age-old Bible verse represents the plight of the single-parent family best: *It is more blessed to give than to receive* (Acts 20:35 KJV). You have to learn to give without expectation, because frequently, little comes back. On a positive note, this serves as a reminder that the true meaning of Christmas was never about gifts. Instead, it's about a tiny baby born in a Bethlehem stable sent to save our lost world.

Of course, there were benevolent family members and friends from work or church who realized our circumstances were financially challenging. Sometimes, little blessings like an unexpected gift certificate, a toy for Zach wrapped in colorful paper, or a Christmas sweater for me appeared during the holidays.

At other times, folks got consumed with their own families and the season seemed bleak and lonely. It was then I tried to muster a cheerful face for my boy, who recognized things were not the way they were supposed to be. So, it was for most of those first twenty Christmases my son and I spent together. Along the way, he became an independent young man, moved out, and began a life of his own.

A New Tradition Is Birthed

When Christmas Eve rolled around the following year, an almost- twenty-one-year-old Zach arrived at my door to celebrate our tradition of enjoying the evening together. There was the usual church service, a tree with twinkling lights, and favorite meal.

Plus, there was a new person joining us for our celebration. Larry Claypool, a public-school administrator and never-married bachelor, who was patiently trying to discover the key to my closed-off heart, and slowly winning my son over as well.

Only a couple months earlier, Larry and I were having a fun day away, when he brought up the possibility of marriage in our future. "Never mention the subject again or our relationship will be over," I answered frantically.

Larry's face clouded with confusion, not understanding my response wasn't about him. It was about past heartbreak. I was trapped by fear, terrified of being hurt again. Still, the forty-eight-year-old bachelor had become a stable presence in our lives and celebrating our first Christmas together felt right.

After a candlelight church service, we returned to my apartment to open presents. When Zach finished unwrapping his gifts, his face radiated with excitement as he proudly handed me a small box. I began tearing the decorative paper, expecting a pair of costume earrings or gold-plated bracelet like in years past. His eyes, eager with anticipation, focused intently on me.

A Sparkling Surprise

Lifting the lid of the ivory satin case, I tried to hide my shock. It bore the name of an expensive jewelry store. I could barely swallow an audible gasp when I glanced down and saw a diamond pendant and glittering chain resting in the box's burgundy velvet lining. By now, Zach's deep blue eyes were dancing with unrestrained delight. Apparently, my son understood the importance of giving.

Unfortunately, I had not discovered how to graciously receive, having had little practice. *How much had this necklace cost him?* It looked to be at least a quarter-carat diamond encircled by a thick band of white gold. The unmistakable sparkle of the stone left little doubt it was real, and Zach's ecstatic look confirmed its authenticity.

The delicate pendant was exquisite, but my faithful man-child worked hard for his retail salary and was attending college too. I often felt guilty I couldn't financially assist him more in achieving his educational and career goals.

The Season's Most Valuable Lesson

Suddenly, I thought about the Christmas sermon from the year before. Pastor David Sharpes had spoken about accepting gifts with appreciation and graciousness, never offending the giver regardless of what the gift was. It hadn't been challenging that Christmas Eve; my son had given me a small handmade boat made of plywood filled with a few Biblical characters and painted animals a couple inches tall. Understanding how significant Old Testament stories are to me, Zach bought the facsimile set of ancient Noah who had built an ark to survive a catastrophic flood. The miniature wooden set was adorable, but coming from an affordable local shop it wasn't extravagant or expensive. In contrast, staring at the finely-crafted necklace, I was faced with accepting something that seemed too much.

Aware of my concern, Zach began telling the story of the gift's origin, a tender tale about a co-worker his age who was a single mom with a toddler. Needing extra cash, she decided to sell the diamond pendant. It was originally a gift to her from a former boyfriend, and no longer possessed any sentimental value. Zach simply purchased it to help her make ends meet and to bless me with an incredible Christmas present.

The diamond sparkled brighter as I gazed at the glistening gold necklace with new appreciation. Instantly, I realized Zachary had seen our lives and struggles replicated in the life of a fellow employee who was also a college student like I had been when he was just a baby. My gift was a visible witness that he had learned the most valuable lesson the holidays can teach, it truly is more blessed to give than to receive.

Larry sat quietly while Zach and I shared this intimate moment between a single mother and her adult child. Not one to give up though, not long after, my gentle suitor asked my son if he could have his permission to marry me. Zach's reply took me by surprise, when he told Larry he needed his support too. This sort of cinched the deal.

By Valentines Day, I owned another diamond in the form of a sparkling engagement ring. That June, we became a family of three, now keeping our annual Christmas tradition quite similar to the very first one together.

Still, I doubt there could ever be another present under the tree able to match the blessing I felt the Christmas when I received the diamond necklace from my beloved boy. After all, even though your son grows up to be a good man, one you are immensely proud of, in a mother's heart, he will always be your little boy.

~ 38 ~
Letting Go of Christmas

Rhett Wilson, Sr.

It's always hard to let go of Christmas.

Christmas is the only season when I really enjoy shopping. Most years Black Friday finds me leaving the house hours before the rest of the family is awake. And over the course of that weekend, as Thanksgiving hymns give way to Christmas ones, the Advent season comes alive once again!

For my wife and me, decorating the Christmas tree stands out as one of our favorite experiences. We love unpacking various ornaments and enjoying memories associated with them — a holy family from The Biltmore House on our honeymoon, a small Ryman Auditorium from Nashville, a beautiful ornament replicating the barn at The Billy Graham Library in Charlotte, and a red ball with the inscription "Thomas Road Baptist Church" which we bought to remind us of our December-trips to Lynchburg, Virginia.

Our family enjoys reading books about Christmas. One series explains from a Christian perspective the traditions of the candy cane, the Christmas stocking, the Christmas tree, and the history of Saint Nicholas. It's as if society adjusts for one month to remember and celebrate what happened at Bethlehem.

The word "Christmas" literally means the mass of Christ, or the worship service about Jesus.

This is the season when people take time to be friendlier and show generosity, compassion, and goodwill by doing things like sharing goods with the hungry and purchasing toys for children in need.

Church services abound with songs about Jesus, festive lights and colors, and genuine wishes of cheer and blessing to one another. Dickens said, "I have always thought of Christmas as a good time; a kind, forgiving, generous, pleasant time; a time when men and women seem to open their hearts freely, and so I say, God bless Christmas!"

For me, the few days before and after Christmas offer time to devote almost completely to my family. For my wife and I, that may be the best gift of all. To have a few days to spend in almost uninterrupted leisure together — that is surely a taste of heaven on earth. Each year I'm surprised how little I long for outside enticements. Email and surfing the internet hold little appeal. I don't want to spend any more money on anything; after the gifts are purchased, there is little pleasure in engaging the outside world of stores, shopping, and the like.

This is when there is time to say, "What do you want to do," and mean it! Time to play long with the children without feeling the need to "hurry it up." Time to engage with them in their world. Time to talk with your spouse and enjoy the blessings of marriage!

Oswald Chambers rightly said that the real test of spiritual maturity is not how well one does on the mountain, but how well he descends the mountain. As we walk forward with the afterglow of Christmas on our backs and still ringing in our ears, may we remember the words of Charles Dickens' Scrooge, "I will honor Christmas in my heart and try to keep it all the year."

~ 39 ~

Putting Christmas Away

Norma C. Mezoe

I've put Christmas away
for another year,
the trimmings and wrappings
and times of good cheer.

The tree, once adorned,
stands shamefully bare
of the tinsel and bulbs
that once hung there with care.

The gifts under the tree
are all stored away;
now little is left
of that wonderful day.

Yet, I'm reminded
that's just one small part.
The important thing is
to keep Christ in my heart.

~ 40 ~

Jesus Christ – the Same Yesterday, Today, and December 26th

Thea Williams

My father-in-law used to say the heaviest thing for him to pick up was a pen. That was back in the days when people used such outdated implements to correspond with each other. Nowadays, we might complain that we can't get ourselves to sit down at the keyboard. Either way, we're talking about writer's block, and mine has been noticeable these last few months.

For me, writing tends to drift even further onto the back burner during the Christmas season. Truth be told, my authorial calling often takes a backseat to the many activities our culture deems necessary to "have ourselves a merry little Christmas."

We do make Christmas ridiculously busy in our society. Not surprisingly, we become tired and cranky, turning what should be a joyous celebration of imperial birth into a time of stress and often emptiness. My own cycle goes something like this:

I begin to get the Christmas spirit before Thanksgiving. I wait eagerly for local radio stations to start playing round-the-clock holiday music, and wade through my disorganized collection of CDs to supplement the radio's somewhat limited offerings. I gradually decorate the house until one day I walk downstairs and realize my vinyl Christmas tablecloth is just *too much* and secretly look forward to stashing it away till next year. When my children were younger, I read Christmas stories and *the* Christmas story to them at bedtime; now that they're grown, I read heartwarming yule tales to myself, without telling anyone (until now). Scented candles make my artificial tree smell piney, and I enjoy them while watching holiday favorites for the thousandth time and munching cheater's Pillsbury cookies out of the freezer (they don't need to be baked; no point wasting time).

I hail from mixed lineage, so we celebrate Hanukkah as well as Christmas. This is one of my favorite parts of the holiday celebration, as it reminds me of my dear father, whose menorah (wax-encrusted and in dire need of polishing, but nevertheless quite functional) almost makes it seem like he's still with us. I send out holiday cards in batches, wending my way through dilapidated address books and church directories. Throughout the month I package up homemade goodies (often "ghost-baked" by my two "elves" — a neighbor and a sister — whose confections are listed right next to nectar and ambrosia on the official menu for the gods), and deliver said treats to deserving service providers, whose goodwill I hope to maintain in the new year.

Somewhere around the 20th I start to panic, realizing I haven't wrapped a thing, let alone finished shopping. I make desperate efforts to complete my purchases and begin wrapping with abandon. Toward the end of the tape roll (and my patience),

I switch over to bagging, which is more sensible anyway, since my boys have zero appreciation for ribbons, bows, or Thomas Kinkade-themed paper.

December 24th is my favorite day of the year, and I try to enjoy it to the fullest. I finish whatever is left to do in the way of gifting or cooking, often visit with family and friends, and generally savor the expectancy of the day. I treasure going to church on Christmas Eve, feeling the warmth in my heart glow brighter with the singing of each cherished hymn. After circling the tree with gifts, I settle down to watch Scrooge or George Bailey evolve into the men God intends them to be, while offering up silent thanks for the many blessings in my life.

Before I know it, Christmas day has arrived, with all its wonderful chaos. Some expectations are met, while other longings remain. One thing I can always count on: it goes too fast. While I'm always relieved that the mad rush is over, I usually also feel a bit of loss — the end of excitement and forward-looking. The realization that winter is upon us, with all its dark, dreary days, tax season looms, and no amount of twinkling lights can make those realities go away. In short, a sense that the fun is over, and it's time to get back to work.

No matter how old I get, I can't seem to make the after-Christmas doldrums go away. I count the days till it's time to go back to work and bite my nails the night before vacation ends. I usually try to stretch out the last day as much as possible, pretending the dawn won't come, and with it, the inevitable jolt back to ordinary life.

Through it all, I try to stick close to God, remembering it is

He whose Son we are celebrating. Still, I wake up the day after New Years tired, overstuffed with food and frolicking, till one thing catches me up short.

Jesus is right where I left Him.

> *Jesus Christ is the same yesterday and today and forever.*
> Hebrews 13:8

~ 41 ~

The Lambing Season

Susan M. Watkins

Today marked the day that people across the globe celebrated the most important birthday on earth.

As I scrambled out of the warmth of my bed, I dashed into our decorated living room to plug in the lights of our tree, and was embraced by the scent of fresh pine. Squeals of delight filled the quiet room as I climbed over the wrapped bounty surrounding our shimmering tree. Mom had a talent for finding unadvertised sales that her children benefitted from annually.

Hours earlier our extended family had surrounded our dinner table for our traditional Polish *Wigilia* Christmas Eve dinner. Foods reserved for this day alone, spilled over onto every available surface that represented our heritage and the holiness of the night.

Fortunately for us, Mom loved to cook and bake. She lived for the heat of the kitchen. Long before the VCR, every Saturday found me alongside our resident chef feverishly copying down televised recipes to catch every ingredient or step that flashed onscreen. It taught me accuracy under pressure.

Planning Christmas Eve dinner was an event unto itself. Weeks of food shopping from specialty and regular grocers, retrieving pots, pans and rarely-seen dishes, and being her sous-chef was the holiday standard. From an early age I proudly stood at my Grammy's cutting board dicing and slicing the way I envisioned she must have done when alive.

Mom was a born chef, at home in a busy kitchen just like her mom had been. Grammy had immigrated here and started her own catering business in the 1930s. It had been unprecedented for a woman, but given her determination and skill, countless people had enjoyed her recipes.

Now, traditional Polish appetizers, soups, entrees, and desserts were prepared for our longstanding dinner. Our refrigerator was woefully inadequate for this bounty; its light no longer discernable, and a firm door closure required.

In honor of Christ's birth, the evening's festivities couldn't start until the first star of the night appeared in the sky; reminiscent of the three wise men on their journey to Bethlehem. I was the designated lookout, and I wouldn't be impeded by snow regardless of how many feet carpeted the ground. After I announced the star's presence, the celebrating began with each family member breaking off a corner of *opłatek*, a thin sheet of wafer, to share with each other while speaking a blessing to them until everyone partook. A twelve-course meal filled our plates as we ate the same menu as previous generations. The table setting included a small bundle of hay resting along the table's edge covered with the corner of the tablecloth, symbolizing Jesus' birth in the stable. An extra place setting was laid with an empty chair to represent Christ's presence among us.

Following weeks of preparing, ingesting, chatting, and

laughing — compliments were generously given for Mom's culinary expertise. And while Dad's compliment was heartfelt, it was her brother's that held generational meaning, because my uncle grew up at Grammy's table. A simple, "That was delicious, kid. Tasted just like Ma's!" refueled her until the next Christmas.

Nobody ever left Mom's table hungry and no one departed without leftovers.

After exchanging gifts with extended family, and mutually telling cousins what their presents were in advance, it was time for our favorite event without Mom or my aunt. They happily stayed home, sipped fresh coffee, visited in quiet with their feet up, and addressed the kitchen's disorder "later."

Dad, my uncle, and all of the cousins bundled up and climbed into my uncle's station wagon, *The Blue Beast*, for a wonderful time with the dads. A snowy drive took us into the heart of our city, known for its lavish Christmas decorations and department store animatronic window vignettes . . . and where we were given new seasonal memories. Dad and my uncle were childhood friends who, with a wink at each other, knew the plan without even speaking.

Our downtown event wasn't a leisurely review; we'd already seen the decorations several times since Thanksgiving. No, this was a fathers-only extravaganza for their offspring. A welcomed experience that loosely heeded the maternal warnings of, "Be careful!" as we raced out the door.

Driving to the end of the first street, my uncle yelled over his shoulder, "Hang on!" We did, mostly to each other, as the car sped up and down hills while red and green streaked past our fogged windows. Laughing and screaming, we all wore ourselves out for the last part of Christmas Eve.

The night wasn't complete without attending Midnight Mass after we said goodbye to family while throwing snowballs at each other.

Our family worshipped year-round in the cavernous century-old church that had been erected with generational craftsmanship inside and out.

It was especially beautiful at Christmastime when two twenty-five-foot evergreen trees flanked the ornately carved gold altar. Waves of poinsettias blanketed their skirts, candle flames danced in their holders, while the scent of pine and incense wafted through the nave, welcoming the faithful.

After we finished singing Christmas carols, the echoing organ introduced our pastor, who retold the Bethlehem account of how, over several days, Joseph and Mary made the ninety-mile trek to Bethlehem with her riding a donkey.

As he spoke, I would slide down and rest my head against the back of the pew to stare at the ornate ceiling far above, trying to visualize the difficult road in my young mind. It was here that I had my first taste of the sacred and was officially introduced to God's Son, Immanuel.

* * * * *

Why did God plan His redemptive blueprint this particular way? There had been no need where God daily walked with Adam and Eve in the cool of the day. On earth as it is in heaven. At least, there had been no need until things took a turn with free will. With the bite and swallow of the forbidden fruit everything changed — except the Lord's immovable love for each of us.

The forbidden fruit penned Christ's birth announcement. That disobedient swallow required redemption, and at the precise timing for bridge building that would sweep the earth in its preparation, a young virgin from Nazareth surrendered to her calling. Mother and holy child grew simultaneously and matched heartbeats.

The little family traveled to Bethlehem for their appointed time. What surprises did they experience along the way? Where did they sleep? They must have slept on the ground while Jesus kicked and stretched to get comfortable . . . the Creator of all things seen and unseen, never hindered or confined, now cramped within His mother.

There were no reservations for a comfortable bed, food, or bath. Bethlehem was indeed crowded as travelers clamored for anywhere to eat and sleep. How concerned Joseph had to have been watching his wife at such an uncomfortable time! In lodging amongst the animals, Mary prepared to meet the deity that Gabriel earlier foretold.

So many challenges for this trio, yet each of them required unwavering obedience for success . . . not the unsteady behavior seen in the Garden of Eden. This time there could be no questioning.

Beyond the manger, shepherds dotted the fields keeping vigilant watch over restless flocks that silent night.

My child's mind thought of lambing season in Israel. Had hundreds of heavily-pregnant ewes and one chosen virgin simultaneously labored to birth their lambs?

Had Judean shepherds helped ewes deliver lambs while Joseph and Mary delivered the holy Lamb of God?

All of heaven must have leaned in for a glimpse of the One who had left their realm only months earlier, the Savior of the world and lover of our souls who now entered our struggle. The weight of redemption rested heavily on this celestial newborn, for eternity is endless, and the Lord couldn't bear to be without us sharing His home.

A sudden explosion of brilliant light and ethereal glory must have engulfed the night skies as an angel announced the good news about Christ's birth . . . identifying Him by mission, name, attire, and location before myriads of angels joined him. They worshipped the Almighty at the long-awaited news of reconciliation between Father God and His children.

Did the infant Jesus hear them in His divinity?

With angelic directions in hand, the herdsmen's journey to Bethlehem ensued. They found the Messiah exactly as His heavenly host had proclaimed. Amidst the curious stable animals as the prophesied Child was revealed, A.D. separated from B.C.

*****

After the service that Christmas Eve, as we drove home on empty streets while the falling snow was pushed aside by the car's windshield wipers, I reflected about all I'd experienced, but especially about being in the Lord's home for the holidays. It was always welcoming with an unearthly beauty and presence.

Once snuggled in bed that wintery night, I felt heaven's hug and my resolve to reside with my Redeemer in His eternal home was unwavering. I drifted off into well-earned sleep, too tired to think about presents.

Christmas morning, though, my excitement roused my sleepy siblings, and I ran to awaken our exhausted parents. A very late night of our Polish celebration, singing and worshipping at church late into the night, and wrapping gifts into the wee hours left little time to recharge.

The aroma of freshly brewed coffee permeated our home, while Mom fixed mugs of homemade hot chocolate with marshmallows for her little flock. Our family settled around our shimmering tree. Favorite Christmas music found its way to our record player, and was soon drowned out by laughing, shrieking, and the sound of tearing wrapping paper.

Whenever I discovered my hoped-for favorite gifts, I'd cross the pandemonium to climb up into my parents' laps for hugs and kisses of gratitude.

Fearlessly returning across the obscured floor, I'd inspect and celebrate my siblings' gifts as they did mine. Our parents were equally gracious over their receipt of our presents; further teaching us by example.

Our excitement spilled over during breakfast and the impatience for assembling new toys.

The rest of the holiday was spent playing and nibbling on leftovers. I could never understand why each year it always felt like a decade was wedged in between the annual calendar pages.

It felt like we'd spent that past year crossing off the days while waiting for Christmastime and then, barely after its arrival, it was breaking the sound barrier with its unwelcomed departure.

We never want Christmas to end, do we? Christmas Eve and

Christmas Day are the crowning pinnacle of every year.

When we celebrate Jesus' birth we open gifts from one another, oddly not giving gifts to The Christ as the Magi did over two millennia ago.

Christ's deep love is that of an inexhaustible giver who wrapped His life in His father's majesty, to be incrementally unwrapped by each of us over our lifetimes. Imagine the immeasurable joy if we gave our lives as Christmas gifts to the holy Lamb born for our restoration and permanence in heaven. The rewards are literally in and out of this world.

Immanuel. God with us. The scope of His name is staggering. The majesty profound. The power immeasurable. The holiness indescribable. Human language is inadequate to capture His omnipotence, and yet the Apostle John who walked, talked, ate, witnessed, and personally experienced Christ, was able to define Him: "God is love."

A triad of simple words that are bottomless and infinite. Not just "God loves us," but God is the very nature and essence of love. Once encountered, we can never be the same.

For God so loved that He gave . . . .

The final reconciliation of lambing season.

About the Authors

Victoria Barker (M.A., Ph.D.) is a graduate of Carson-Newman and The University of Tennessee, Knoxville. She is a Professor Emerita at Carson-Newman University in Jefferson City, Tennessee, where she teaches classes in American Literature and Literature for Young Adults. She has been a curriculum writer for Lifeway Resources of the Southern Baptist Convention and has published and presented articles on Kentucky literature for a number of years.

Victoria, a native of Kentucky who has lived in East Tennessee for over 50 years, is active in her church, teaching an adult class and singing in the choir. She enjoys travel, gardening, and genealogy. She and her husband, Sheridan, are the parents of an adult son and daughter and have three grandchildren.

Dee Bowlin's diverse, award-winning poetry has been published in *Artemis, Encore, Golden Words, Red Earth Revisited, Answering the Call,* and *Virginia Literary Journal*. She published her first book, *Finding Splendid Shelter: A Memoir with Poetry and Photographs,* in 2024. Her songs have been performed on stage, and she has received honors for her photography.

Dee is a member of the Poetry Society of Oklahoma and Roanoke Valley Christian Writers. She lives in the Roanoke Valley of Virginia, where the Blue Ridge Mountains, the squirrels, and the songbirds greet her every morning.

Sue Briggs always loved reading and when she was young she thought she might like to work in publishing or even be a writer. Her mother quickly forbade this though, telling her that all writers were "weird." She began to write as a hobby, then after her daughter left home Sue took some writing courses at the community college in her hometown, and later joined a writers group. For about 25 years she volunteered in a ministry to developmentally disabled people at her church. She left that ministry after she and her husband retired from working for the State of Michigan and moved to a different town to be closer to family. Sue continues to write and has had a few things published, though writing has remained her hobby, not a profession.

Wendy C. Brown is a seeker and lover of nature who also enjoys writing, teaching, speaking, photography, and checking out the wild side of life. She is married with three beautiful adult children and one awesome daughter-in-law.

Wendy has a heart for the tiniest flames of passion to burst into reality. She brings the ability to infuse excitement, hope, and practical possibilities into even the most challenging situations. As a professional marriage and family therapist, writer, storyteller, and speaker, she brings her whole heart to understand, connect, guide, entertain, and inspire. Wendy has ghostwritten several books, taught at writers' conferences, and released her own work, titled *Single Wives: How to Thrive in a Disconnected Marriage*.

Christina Ryan Claypool is a former TV reporter/producer, past award-winning newspaper columnist, and author of *Secrets of the Pastor's Wife: A Novel*. As a teenager, she supernaturally survived a near fatal suicide attempt and was confined to a state mental institution. Following continued hospitalizations and several more serious suicide attempts, Christina finally found salvation in Jesus on a psychiatric ward in 1986. Since then, she has learned to live in recovery one day at a time through her Savior's healing power. She has been featured on CBN's 700 Club and Joyce Meyer Ministries TV program sharing her miraculous testimony. Christina graduated from Bluffton University and earned a Master of Arts in Ministry from Mount Vernon Nazarene University in 2005. Learn more at www.christinaryanclaypool.com.

Karen Cook, a softlines merchandiser and volunteer associate minister, is working on a memoir of her life including the spiritual aspects of mental illness.

She and her husband, Greg, are adjusting to their newly-empty nest in Walker, Michigan, and are very grateful their little birdies, Maddie and Sophie, haven't flown very far away. Karen and Greg like traveling, bike riding, sampling new restaurants, and finding fun things to do with their "girls." Her life verse is Jeremiah 23:11-13.

Ben Cooper is a Christian, husband, father, author, speaker, beekeeper, home missionary, and more. Growing up on a family farm, earning an Agricultural Science degree from Penn State University, working 32 years for Maryland Department of Agriculture, and being a beekeeper has allowed him to spend much of his time around animals and nature. He uses those experiences as the basis for writing his books, other stories in the Divine Moments series, and for Guideposts annual devotional *All God's Creatures*. He resides among the foot slopes of the eastern Continental Divide in southern Pennsylvania. Contact him at cooperville@breezeline.net.

Barbara D'Antoni Diggs is the author of *Suppose I Hadn't Listened*, a collection of 40 heart-warming, true stories from some of her most memorable mission experiences around the world. She has published articles for several magazines, and in anthologies *Short and Sweet, Divine Moments*, and *Chicken Soup for the Soul*. She loves visiting with people from other countries and trying to learn words in their language. While she enjoys reading and writing, she feels her present call is to encourage, pray for, and cheer on the careers of Christian authors as they write their books. She and her husband make their home in east Tennessee.

Jan Elder writes Christian romance and cozy mysteries. She strives to write the kind of book that strengthens the reader's faith, while also providing an entertaining and engrossing love story. Two of her eight published novels have won International Digital awards.

In addition to writing, she craves the occasional caramel Frappuccino and is a devoted watcher of Turner Classic Movies. Every novel she writes features a feline in some way.

Happily married for over 20 years, she and husband, Steve, live at the gateway to western Maryland with Kassie Rae (an elegant, mini black panther), and Looney Tunes (a silly tuxedo cat.) Look for Jan's books at: https://janelderauthor.com.

Terri Elders, LCSW, a lifelong writer and editor, has contributed to over 150 anthologies. After a quarter-century odyssey, including a decade overseas with Peace Corps, eleven years ago she finally returned to her native California where she lives not far from her beloved Pacific Ocean. Her stories have been published in multiple copies of the Divine Moments series.

Bonnie Evans is a Christian communicator whose words offer hope to those feeling weary and invisible. Drawing from seasons littered with depression and fear, Bonnie shares how God walked with and fought for her as He delivered the comfort, strength, and spiritual weapons needed for each battle.

Since 1982, she has encouraged others through magazine articles, weekly newspaper columns, Bible studies, workshops, and eight published books. Her writing invites readers to discover God's presence in their own stories — especially in the darkest chapters. With intentional vulnerability, she assures us that we are known, tended, and loved by a God who intimately understands every sentence of our story.

Stacey Longo Graham's childhood fascination was the written word. Forget toys; she wanted books. After years as an attorney working in child welfare law, she embraced her lifelong passion — writing. However, instead of hiking in dense woods, swimming in open water, strolling along a shoreline, reading a book, attending small town festivals, and anticipating retirement with her husband; she's now driving carpool, checking homework, watching soccer practices, and being a mom to a child she never saw coming. Inspirational writing is her gift to them both. She's celebrating this season of life with wit, empathy, laughter, tears, mistakes, and teachable moments.

Judy Harman was born and raised in the Blue Ridge Mountains of Virginia. She received a teaching degree from Longwood College, and taught 3rd grade in Roanoke City until stopping to be home more with her husband, Jim, and their two children. After suddenly becoming a widow 24 years ago, she has since marveled at the opportunities God has given her to travel, speak, mentor, and teach women of all ages and varied nationalities.

Judy recently retired from being the Director of Women's Ministries at her church, but continues to be burdened for the encouragement and spiritual growth of women. She is currently writing her memoirs from her home in the Roanoke Valley.

Joanna K. Harris grew up as a missionary kid with a love for stories and a dream of being a missionary. After Bible College, she served in Mexico for two years. During that time, she felt called to write. Then, God took her on an unexpected journey of more than a decade of chronic illness.

Through her suffering, Jesus taught her more about His grace — always greater than our need. Now, she serves as a "media missionary," encouraging others through writing, editing, and coaching. Joanna has authored more than a dozen books for children and adults. She believes every day is better with a good book, dark chocolate, laughing with friends, and an awareness of God's ever-present grace. Connect with her on her website at www.gracepossible.com.

Lydia E. Harris, M.A. in home economics, is blessed with five grandchildren and is known as "Grandma Tea." She writes the column, "A Cup of Tea with Lydia," and is the author of three books for grandparents, all available on amazon: *Preparing My Heart for Grandparenting; In the Kitchen with Grandma: Stirring Up Tasty Memories Together;* and *GRAND Moments: Devotions Inspired by Grandkids.*

Sharilynn Hunt, DMin, is a retired medical social worker and former founder of New Creation Realities Ministry. She has authored inspirational stories for several local anthologies and Chicken Soup for the Soul's *Best Mom Ever!*, *The Forgiveness Fix, All You Need Is Love*, and *Hope, Faith & Miracles*, Bethany House *Life-Changing Miracles* and *Heaven Sightings*, and Guideposts *Miracles Do Happen* and *Divine Interventions*. Her books, *Grace Overcomes Today* and *Together WE Pray (How to Have Effective Prayer Groups)*, are sold on Amazon.

Shari and her husband live in Tennessee. They have two children, and four grandchildren. They love to travel and have almost reached their goal of visiting all 50 U.S. states. She enjoys scrapbooking their trips and doing jigsaw puzzles in her spare time.

Tina Hurdt loves her Savior, His Word, and His constant presence in her life's journeys. She lives her life through eyes of laughter, finding comfort in "counting it all joy." She is most appreciative of the family God has gifted her.

Her stories have been published in the church publication *Christmas Joys*. She is currently working on two new endeavors: *Prosthetic Parables – Life Stories of an Amputee* and *This Is the Day He Became Real*.

Tina firmly believes that sharing the difficult times can offer inspiration to others, and prays her writings will bring a little laughter, encouragement, and perspective to those whose paths they cross.

Carmen Leal is a storyteller and the author of 12 books including *When Love Wags a Tail* and *I Chose You, Imperfectly Perfect Rescue Dogs and Their Humans*, numerous articles, devotionals, and human-interest stories. Carmen's faith, wit, humor, and poignant personal observations, coupled with her down-to-earth style and common-sense approach to dealing with life, make her a popular presenter as she inspires and motivates others. Carmen and her husband relocated from Hawaii to Oshkosh where she has become an awesome dog mom and a reluctant gardener who knows a crazy amount about Wisconsin weeds.

J.J. LeVan is a wife and mother to a blended, growing family of five adults. Her oldest son was diagnosed with PDD/NOS, autism, in 1998. She has since become an advocate and writer for autism, as well as a Certified Independent Provider for people with special needs.

She enjoys spending time with her family in Ohio and drinking fierce, black coffee. She can often be found in her basement sharking around their pool table or out in the wild, dominating the backseat of her husband's Honda Goldwing. She is the award-winning author of the children's picture book *He Meant You to be You*.

Sherri R. Mewha is an author, blogger, speaker, and Bible teacher. After decades in the corporate world, she was convicted of the need for Christian women to follow Christ's example in teaching, discipling, and serving one another.

During the ten years that she established and led the women's ministry program in a local church, Sherri began writing and teaching

Bible studies, programs, and devotions. In 2022, she started focusing full-time on writing, speaking, and blogging.

Sherri is a Christ-follower, Bible-lover, wife, mom, and Mimi of five beautiful grandchildren whose calling and great is to joy to write, teach, and talk to women about our awesome God and His Word.

Norma C. Mezoe has been a published writer for 40 years. Her writing has appeared in books, devotionals, take-home papers and magazines. She writes to honor God, to encourage, and to point others to the Lord. Norma became a Christian at the age of 15 but didn't grow spiritually in a significant way until a crisis, at the age of 33, brought her into a closer relationship with the Lord. She can be contacted at: normacm@tds.net.

Maureen Miller is an award-winning author with stories in more than 20 collaboratives. She contributes to Guideposts' *All God's Creatures*, her local newspaper, and several online devotion sites, including the award-winning *Arise Daily* and *Inspire a Fire*.

Married for 36 years to her childhood sweetheart Bill, she enjoys life with their three born-in-their-hearts children and three grand-girls, not to mention a variety of furry beasts. They live on Selah Farm, a hobby homestead nestled in the mountains of western North Carolina.

Maureen blogs at *Windows and Wallflowers*, telling of God's extraordinary character discovered in the ordinary things of life: (Maureenmillerauthor.com). Her debut novel is *Gideon's Book*.

Vicki H. Moss is former Editor-at-Large and Contributing Editor for *Southern Writers Magazine* and former pundit for the *American Daily Herald*. A workshop instructor for writing conferences, Vicki teaches from her books *How to Write for Kids' Magazine* and *Writing with Voice*. With 800 articles published, she co-authored the book *nailed It!* and contributed to Cecil Murphey's book, *I Believe in Heaven*. A poet, blogger, speaker, free-lance editor, and ghostwriter, Vicki also makes school author visits. Author of *Adrift, Smelling Stinkweed, Rogue Hearts,* and two poetry books *Roisin Dubh* and *Porch Pickin' People,* she's published articles and poems in Scotland's *Thistle Blower, Country Woman, Christian Devotions, In the City, Hopscotch, Fun for Kidz, Boys' Quest,* and has written 40 stories for the Divine Moments series.

Ane Mulligan has been a voracious reader ever since her mother instilled within her a love of books at age three. Together, they would escape into worlds otherwise unknown. Then, when Ane saw *Peter Pan* on stage, she was struck by a fever and never recovered — stage fever. Now, by night she wears a director's hat at a community theatre and by day she's a bestselling, award-winning novelist.

Ane lives in Sugar Hill, Georgia, with her artist husband, a rescued German Shepherd, and a rascally Rottweiler. Find Ane on her website, Facebook, The Write Conversation, and the Blue Ridge Conference Blog.

Suzanne Dodge Nichols is published in three of Grace Publishing's *Divine Moments Christmas* anthologies and eight of the *Short and Sweet* anthologies. Her writings are featured in three compilations published by the Southern Christian Writers Conference. Suzanne is the author of *Transplant the Iris*, a memoir honoring her maternal grandparents. She is a co-author of five volumes of *COFFEE with God*. Several compositions in various genres have earned her first and second place writing awards.

Suzanne and her husband live in north Alabama. They have three children and 11 grandchildren who live *much* too far away.

Brenda Poinsett works with adults who want to learn, with families who want meaningful celebrations, and with women who are interested in missions. Offering encouragement, inspiration, ideas, and valuable information, Brenda speaks at conferences, leads a missions group, and writes curriculum materials and books.

She is the author of 22 books including *Can Martha Have a Mary Christmas?*, *Unwrapping Martha's Joy*, *The Friendship Factor*, *Wonder Women of the Bible*, *When Saints Sing the Blues*, *Celebrations That Touch the Heart*, and *You've Got It, I Want It*. Brenda and her husband, Bob, have three sons and live in east central Missouri.

Connie Pombo is the author of four books, including *Coffee Lover's Devotional: Take a Break from the Daily Grind*, and is contributing author to numerous anthologies, with more than 40 stories appearing in the *Chicken Soup for the Soul* series. She writes to encourage others in their walk of faith, weaving spiritual insights into everyday experiences of family, friendship, and the simple joys of life.

Connie and her husband make their home on Florida's Gulf Coast, where they cherish time with their four grandchildren. Her passion for writing is matched by her love for sharing God's goodness in ordinary moments. Learn more about her work at conniepombo.com.

April G. Pope and her husband JW live and work on their farm that borders the Cape Fear River in central North Carolina. There they primarily raise beef cattle and Gypsy Vanner horses. April enjoys her role as shepherdess to a flock of Katahdin sheep who serve as her inspiration for weekly devotions called *Pasture Parables*.

Off the farm, her life as a family medicine Physician Assistant and Campbell University faculty member, keeps her busy, but when time allows, April loves to saddle up a horse and ride on the farm. She loves photographing their farm life, working with livestock guardian dogs, and cooking.

Learn more about April and her farm life on FaceBook and InstaGram @ Cape Fear FarmLife.

Anne Foley Rauth has been featured in *Chicken Soup for the Soul*, Guideposts' *Angels on Earth* magazine, *Standard*, Guideposts' monthly magazine, Focus on the Family, and other publications. Well-seasoned in the fields of marketing, promotion, and advertising, she has worked at Hallmark and H&R Block. She is currently a fractional Chief Development Officer for nonprofits.

Anne and her husband own an Airbnb in Missouri used for writing and quilting retreats (https://airbnb.com/h/-quilt-retreat-oasis). She's mom of three Eagle Scouts.

Anne writes to remind the rejected that they're remembered, restored, and relentlessly loved. Serving on the Advisory Board of the Heart of America Christian Writers' Network, she loves hearing new ideas on how to encourage writers. Connect with her on LinkedIn: https://www.linkedin.com/in/annerauth/ or at annerauth.com.

Lorilyn Roberts is an award-winning author who has contributed to or authored over 20 books, including the *Seventh Dimension Series*. She graduated Magna Cum Laude from the University of Alabama, and later earned a Master of Arts in Creative Writing from Perelandra

College. Her latest book, *Eighth Dimension - Frequency* for Young Adults was released in September 2025.

Xavia Arndt Sheffield has written music, lyrics, comedy, poetry, devotionals and a Bible Study titled *Life Principles From the Women of Acts*. Her devotionals have appeared in *The Upper Room*, *These Days*, and on-line for the Washington National Cathedral for Advent and Lent. Her writing has also appeared in *Monday Morning* and *Presbyterians Today* magazines.

As a Presbyterian minister's wife of 40 years, she has been involved in most aspects of church life, including teaching women of the Bible and other classes, creating Sunday School Kick-off Programs, serving as Children's Music Director, and creating over 1,000 bulletin boards. She holds a BA in Music and an MA in Speech/Theater from SDSU. She and her husband have a daughter and a son.

David Sowards is a novelist, poet, local TV show host, juggler, magician, songwriter, musician, stand up comedian, short story writer, freelance writer, self syndicated writer, guitar player, piano player, and record producer. His works are widely available on the Internet. He lives in Fort Wayne, Indiana where he is also involved in volunteer work helping others.

Annmarie B. Tait resides in Harleysville, Pennsylvania with her husband Joe Beck. She has stories published in several volumes of *Chicken Soup for the Soul, Patchwork Path, the HCI Ultimate* series, *Reminisce Magazine,* and the Blue Mountain Press publication *Irish Inspirations*. In addition to writing tales about growing up in her large Irish-Catholic family and the memories they made, Annmarie also cultivates a passion for cooking, crocheting, Scrabble and as of late, "Wordle." She also enjoys singing and recording Irish and American Folk Songs. You can contact Annmarie at irishbloom@aol.com.

Cecil Taylor has a passion for helping families and has taught youth and adults in his church and beyond for over 30 years, leading small groups, parenting classes, Bible studies, and retreats.

Cecil Taylor Ministries offers video lessons, books, study guides, podcasts, blogs, and speaker services to help churches, small groups, and individual learners in living a seven-day practical faith. He hosts the *Practical Faith Academy* podcast. His book, *Unison Parenting*, has its own website: UnisonParenting.com.

Married for 40 years, Cecil is father to three adult children. He loves sports (especially his Texas Longhorns), plays fantasy football, and enjoys pin collecting, gardening, and landscaping.

He has been published previously in Grace Publishing's *Lost... and Found*. Visit his website at CecilTaylorMinistries.com.

Leigh Ann Thomas loves to live joyfully and encourage others to seek God's best. She has penned four books including *Smack-Dab in the Midlife Zone: Inspiration for Women in the Middle* and *Ribbons, Lace, and Moments of Grace — Inspiration for the Mother of the Bride*. A contract writer for Salem Web Network (*Christianity.com, BibleStudyTools.com, Crosswalk.com*, etc.), she has also written for *Arise Daily Devotions, ChristianDevotions.us, Southern Writers Suite T, Power for Living*, and more. Leigh Ann is married to her sweetheart, Roy, and they are thankful for the gifts of three daughters, two sons-in-law, and six amazing grandchildren. Connect with her at LeighAThomas.com.

Kay S. Walsh retired from teaching in the psychology department at James Madison University. She views psychology as the discovery of what God created. She and her husband are grateful for their adult children and young grandchildren. They recently added a three-year-old dog to their household, a Labrador named Mango.

Kay led the Shenandoah Christian Writers in Virginia for over 15 years. She typically writes short, non-fiction stories that illustrate God's involvement in our personal lives. She has published articles in magazines and compilation books, including several published by Guideposts. She assisted in editing and writing a book of stories by the members of the Shenandoah Christian Writers titled *The Hope Feathers: Finding Refuge Beneath His Wings*.

Susan M. Watkins is an award-winning multi-published author who interviewed guests and wrote for the CBN's worldwide television program *The 700 Club*. Her work is featured in numerous books, a variety of CBN's global websites, and has appeared in major newspapers.

She has penned several columns, one voted Best of the Best. Additional collaborative credits include Grammy Award winner Gloria Gaynor's *We Will Survive* and a Max Lucado evangelistic website.

Entering her initial writing competition at age eleven, Susan secured first place and ignited her passion as a surrendered scribe. She is described as "a literary artist painting with the stroke of a pen" whose readers immerse themselves in her vibrant storytelling.

Lori Williams is a freelance writer and public speaker whose most creative ideas arise from hanging out with preschoolers. She loves to serve as pianist at her church, teach music to four and five-year-olds on Wednesday nights, and raise swallowtail caterpillars who eat all the dill in her herb garden before turning into butterflies.

She is currently working on two book projects: A devotional titled *Wide-Eyed Worship* and a children's picture book titled *Cantaloupe Moon*. Contact Lori at lawordwright@gmail.com.

Thea Williams is "Mom" to two adult sons and "Mom Mom" to four much-loved grandchildren. She is a retired educator and home health aide who still enjoys assisting disabled individuals in her church and community. She loves cuddling and cooing to her grandkids, teaching the Bible, reading, and serving the Lord.

Thea's published work includes a young adult novel, *Belabored*, available on Amazon; inclusion of her short story, "Phoenix," in *50 Over Fifty: A Celebration of Established and Emerging Women Writers*, also available on Amazon; and articles in various periodicals. Check out more of Thea's writing at www.reflectionsbythea.blogspot.com.

Rhett Wilson, Sr., a professional communicator, loves telling stories, connecting great ideas with people. He has served as Senior Writer for the Billy Graham Evangelistic Association, Senior Communications Director for Leighton Ford Ministries, and writes and edits for others through his business, Hendrix Communications. He and his wife Tracey live in South Carolina. Check out his website at www.rhettwilson.org.

Donna Wyland is an award-winning author and Certified Christian Life and Writing Coach. Her passion is to encourage women toward deeper faith and trust in God as their ultimate source for all things. Her newest release, *Last Best Year — A Short Guide to a Grateful Life*, inspires readers to consider the power of a grateful heart and the legacy they hope to leave behind.

Donna and her husband live in Southwest Florida where they enjoy golfing and spending time with her husband's energetic 96-year-old dad. Donna's award-winning picture books, *'Twas the Night Before Jesus* and *Psalms in Rhyme for Little Hearts*, as well as *Last Best Year* are available on Amazon. Connect with her at https://www.donnawyland.com.

If you enjoyed
'Tis the Season
you might also enjoy these
books in the Divine Moments series
Divine Moments
Christmas Moments
Spoken Moments
Precious, Precocious Moments
More Christmas Moments
Stupid Moments
Additional Christmas Moments
Why? Titanic Moments
Loving Moments
Merry Christmas Moments
Cool-inary Moments
Moments with Billy Graham
Personal Titanic Moments
Remembering Christmas
Romantic Moments
Pandemic Moments
Christmas Stories
Broken Moments
Celebrating Christmas
Grandma's Cookie Jar
Can, Sir!
Christmas Spirit
Joy to the World
Lost . . . and Found
Treasured Moments
A Gift of Love

www.ingramcontent.com/pod-product-compliance
Lightning Source LLC
Chambersburg PA
CBHW060532100426
42743CB00009B/1503